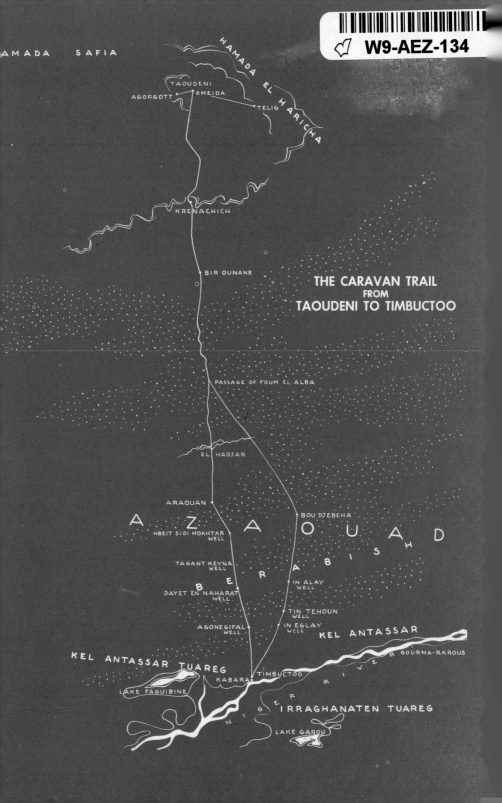

AMADA   SAFIA

HAMADA EL HARICHA

W9-AEZ-134

TAOUDENI
AGORGOTT   SMEIDA
TELIG

KRENACHICH

BIR OUNANE

THE CARAVAN TRAIL
FROM
TAOUDENI TO TIMBUCTOO

PASSAGE OF FOUM EL ALBA

EL HADJAR

ARAOUAN

BOU DJEBEHA

A Z A O U A D

NBEIT SIDI MOKHTAR
WELL

TAGANT KEYNA
WELL

B E R A B I S H

IN ALAY
WELL

DAYET EN NAHARAT
WELL

TIN TEHOUN
WELL

AGONEGIFAL
WELL

IN EGLAY
WELL

KEL ANTASSAR

KEL ANTASSAR TUAREG

KABARA   TIMBUCTOO

N I G E R   R I V E R   GOURMA-RAROUS

LAKE FAGUIBINE

IRRAGHANATEN TUAREG

LAKE GAROU

Azalaï

Azalaï

JOHN SKOLLE

WITH MAPS AND PHOTOGRAPHS BY THE AUTHOR

HARPER & BROTHERS   New York

ACKNOWLEDGMENTS

The author gratefully acknowledges the encouragement he has received from his friends and from his publisher.

Thanks are due to the editors of *The Hudson Review* and *Landscape Magazine* for permission to reprint "The Blue Men" and part of the material on nomads and oases.

CONTENTS

THE SAHARA TODAY

0 100 200 300 400 500
MILES

**SAHARAN TRADING CENTERS
AND CARAVAN JUNCTIONS**
PRIOR TO THE 15th CENTURY

0 100 200 300 400 500
MILES

ONE

THE SEARCH

1   Kasbah

YOU MAY WISH TO GO TO THE MOON. I WAS WILLING TO SETTLE
for Timbuctoo. It took me a long time to get there, but I
finally did, in a roundabout way. Instead of projecting myself into the future, I stepped back into the living past.

It happened by stages.

For some years before the war I lived in the South of
France. There was a spell of magic in the faded villages
and the red earth, the scent of orange blossoms, the sunlight
slanting through the olive trees. The people were friendly

and the wine was good. But what intrigued me most, next to the astounding number of pretty women, was the Arabs who frequently appeared in the cafés. They came to peddle rugs, leather goods, cheap bracelets and, when they thought they could sway a recalcitrant customer with a spark of vice, they played their last trump: a stack of dirty post cards.

This was ordinary enough. The remarkable part about it was that, no matter how hard up they were, they took their constant defeats with supine equanimity; they were un-ruffled by their precarious economic situation. I felt a certain admiration for them. I felt that, underneath the dirty post cards, there was a core of inner pride. Even if they didn't make a sale, these droopy-eyed hawkers were agreeable about answering questions that had nothing to do with business. They had never read a book. They could not read. Yet they expressed themselves in a poetic manner. Among Europeans they never referred to themselves as Arabs; they elected to call themselves *nous autres,* "we others," by voluntary dis-sociation. They were polite toward the stranger, yet they kept aloof. They were poor, but calm in their assurance of the spiritual peace and the carnal delights of the Moslem paradise which their Prophet had promised every true be-liever. They were street Arabs, but it was impressed upon me that even the meanest among them had a touch of nobility.

What kind of a world was it that produced such incon-gruous people?

Sometimes the trees along the shore were lashed by a sirocco and the crisp landscape of southern France was obscured by a strange yellow fog. Clouds of fine particles of sand came racing across the sea from Africa. The frivolous atmosphere of the Côte d'Azur was invaded by a foreign element, a dark power. At such moments I thought of the Sahara, of uninterrupted space that fused into the distant sky without horizon. I disliked caves. I was attracted by the image of a boundless land.

It was not until many years later that I caught my first glimpse of the desert. In the interim I did get as far as Algiers where I found a small native house high above the city, and a beautiful English girl who shared my enthusiasm for North Africa. Together, we explored not only Algiers but the entire region from the fashionable Roman ruins of Tipaza to the amphitheater at Carthage. Nearer to home, we often wandered up into the barren hills with a hamper of champagne and *pâté de foie gras* to enjoy a long view of the Barbary Coast and the sparkling Mediterranean. On one such occasion, when all the world seemed made for our pleasure, a formidable rumbling rent the still afternoon. Before we knew it, a detachment of artillery was upon us and we were in the middle of a military maneuver, the object of which was to take the city of Algiers from the rear. According to plan, Arab soldiers wheeled one of the batteries into a prescribed position right behind us. We had not recovered from our surprise when a young French officer strode up, saluted smartly, and thundered at his men: "What the hell do you think you are doing? Don't you see what's going on here? Move the battery a hundred yards down the hill!"

Then he turned to us and saluted again, smiling, to offer his apologies.

The Arab soldiers understood perfectly. They had an ingrained respect for anyone's privacy. They laughed and joked as they pushed the cannon away from us. Perhaps some of them still tell the story of their gallant officer in the villages.

We loved North Africa.

Below, in town, Arab gentlemen strolled about in white and scarlet robes along the tree-lined avenues. Of course, there was a lot of riffraff, too; peddlers, taxi drivers, stevedores. I wondered what these people were like farther inland. Had the nomads of the Sahara retained a greater degree of integrity? Would they accept a stranger? The men who came out of the desert always had an air of superiority about them, and the storytellers in the square in front of the mosque often extolled their prowess and their virtues as they chanted to the drum beats of a *derbouka* while the rapt listeners repeated the high points of the story or interjected affirmative exclamations in a spontaneous chorus. There was an old man who specialized in a certain romance. Each time he told it, he added a few embellishments. The introduction of the hero would be greeted with approving murmurs of "*Hamdullah*. . . . Praise to God. . . ." and when the old man spoke of the lovely Safia, the ragged audience (having heard the story many times before) repeated after him: "Safia . . . oh Safia . . . moon of my soul. . . ." When he sang about the villain who rode in combat toward her lover "faster than the bullets in the wind," the listeners readily gave voice to their agreement that he had "fire in his eyes and poison in his heart. . . ."

The women of the nomads came to town unveiled and were under less stricture than those of the urban Arabs. I had a demonstration of this in the "blue"-light district of the Kasbah where I had noticed an unusually attractive trio of *filles de joie* who exhibited their charms to all comers in front of their establishment while a coal-black Negro literally drummed up business with a large tom-tom, an engaging grin spread over his syphilitic face. One evening, from a little café across the narrow street, I attempted to make some sketches of the girls. Although I was doing it very discreetly, I hardly got started. They had no sooner noticed what I was up to than they abandoned their alluring poses. With a mixture of shyness and indignation they went inside and slammed the door.

Stern religious principles dominate the behavior of the Arabs. One of them forbids the representation of any form of life.

My idyllic existence in Algiers gradually deteriorated through a chronic lack of funds. I had to "face reality," quite a problem in the circumstances. Among other things I had collected seventeen stray cats which I had christened with the names of all the oases I had hoped to visit: Biskra . . . Ouargla . . . Timimoun. . . .

It was in vain that I tried to apply the philosophy of my aunt, the lion tamer, who used to say: "When things get too tough for you to handle, let them take care of themselves."

Poor soul, one moment she herself forgot that she was in a cage, among ferocious animals.

I had to return to New York and get a job. Then the war came and my personal difficulties seemed insignificant indeed. But through all those dark years the African desert shone brightly in my imagination. I had to wait a long time, yet one day I found myself back in Algiers, wandering through the maze of the Kasbah. In addition to the Rue du Chameau and the Rue du Diable there now was a Rue de la Bombe.

This time Algiers was merely a stopover. I was prepared to brave fate, hardships and bureaucracy to become acquainted with the Tuareg tribesmen, one of the most baffling peoples of Africa.

2   Inquisition

THERE ARE TWO "ROADS" SOUTH ACROSS THE SAHARA. ONE LEADS through the central desert via the oases of Ghardaïa, El-Goléa and In-Salah into the Hoggar Mountains, the heart of the Tuareg country; the other, to the west, connects the Algerian military post Colomb-Béchar with the town of Gao on the Niger River.

On my first trip into the desert I traveled with a friend, a British colonel, who was driving back to his post as district officer in Kenya in his Bedford lorry. I had met him in Ghardaïa, about five hundred miles inland from the Algerian coast, where I was waiting for transportation to Tamanrasset in the Hoggar. The hotel in Ghardaïa was pleasant enough, if expensive. There were a few elderly couples on a conducted tour, a few officers who came and went, and a baby ostrich. The mad confusion of the market place was a mile away.

Among others I had casually met a Frenchman who identified himself as an engineer. He was supervising extensive electrical installations, he said. He was a stocky, square-headed man with steady, unsmiling eyes who spoke fluent Arabic. Considering the importance of his job, he did remarkably little work. His chief occupation consisted of hanging about the bar and strolling in the patio, listening to conversations and asking questions. He was greatly interested in my plans, much more so than I was in his. He never bought a drink but, slyly, persistently, he managed to become part of a group that would sooner or later count him in.

One morning, when my door was ajar, he briskly entered my room without knocking and hung up his hat, saying, "I want you to write a letter for me in English. My sister's husband is English and I want to write him personally in regard to some legal documents."

"All right," I said. "This is rather sudden, but I'll do the best I can."

He hadn't thought of bringing his own stationery, so I got out my writing paper while he looked around the room.

"Is this all the luggage you have?" he asked out of a clear sky.

"Yes," I said, "what about it?"

This made no dent.

"Well, let's get to work," he said as if he had hired me as

his secretary. "Start the letter: 'Dear Tom, I received your message a week ago. I wanted to write you sooner but, as you know, I am very busy here. I trust that Nicole and the children are in good health. . . .' "

"Yes, go on."

My visitor was hypnotizing a fly.

"Are you married?"

"No, not at the moment."

"A trip like yours must cost a pretty penny."

"Oh, you know, nowadays everything is expensive. Do you wish to say something more in your letter?"

"Yes. Continue: 'I expect to see Grandmother in another month or so. Please give my regards to your brother and send me the papers at your earliest convenience.' Now read it back to me."

I carried on the comedy for a few more minutes. Naturally, I could see right through him. It was almost amusing to watch him try to fool me when I knew his game all along. After a while I asked him point-blank: "I suppose what you really want is to see my passport? Is that your business?"

"Yes," he said severely, "I want to see your passport. That is my business."

It occurred to me that he might have demanded it without all this mystery.

He carefully studied every page. He even held the paper against the light, presumably to check watermarks. At one point his wooden face attempted a dreamy expression, as if all the shady characters of his career were passing in review before his penetrating mind.

"How much money do you have?"

I told him, approximately.

The Search · *10*

"What is that over there?"

"My sleeping bag."

"Are you planning to get married again?"

"It's just a single sleeping bag. . . . I mean, yes, possibly."

"How long have you had this passport?"

I told him. "The date is in it, you know."

His face had become hardwood again.

"How long do you intend to stay here?"

"A few days. I had hoped to relax in peace for a while before going farther south."

"You are an artist? What do you paint? Landscapes? Portraits?"

"No," I said, "I prefer to do abstractions; that way I don't have to look at people."

"Abstractions? You mean that cubist stuff? Why don't you paint pretty pictures?"

I let that pass. My inquisitor showed strong disapproval.

"Well," he said, "it doesn't make sense to me. See you later. I'll have to make a report."

A report? What was wrong? Suddenly the whole thing burned me up. I went to see the manager of the hotel.

"Look," I said, "you are trying to run a respectable hotel. Who is the man who constantly sneaks around in the patio? Just now he walked into my room and proceeded to dictate a stupid letter which he wanted me to write for him in English. Then he asked me all kinds of impertinent questions. He even examined my passport and didn't seem to be satisfied with it. I assure you, this is the first time in my life that anyone has doubted my credentials. What is the meaning of all this?"

"Wait a minute," he said. "I believe the police commissioner happens to be in the bar. I'll call him."

The police commissioner was a very agreeable and good-natured gentleman. He listened to my story, thought a moment, then said: "Hum, strange, he is not a police agent. Wanted to see your papers, did he? I shall speak to him. I am very sorry this happened to you. Will you come to my office tomorrow morning?"

A few hours after this interview the impostor came crawling to me. He had changed his tune. I had misunderstood the whole thing, he said. He had only asked me to do him a favor, after all. Wasn't I ashamed to make such a fuss?

"No," I said, "I am not a bit ashamed. No friend of mine has ever posed as a detective and examined my papers. There is no misunderstanding as far as I am concerned, and the less I see of you the better I'll like it."

The fellow was deeply hurt by my harsh attitude.

When I called on the police commissioner, he asked me if the self-styled secret agent had apologized.

"Yes," I said, "I suppose he has in his fashion."

"Well, poor devil, I am sure he really didn't mean any harm. I suspect that he is a little crazy. Why don't you forget the whole thing and send us a lot of tourists from America? Good-by and good luck!"

The next morning, at breakfast, the hotel manager asked me if, by chance, I had any idea of the man's address.

"No," I said, "he didn't give me any information about himself. Why?"

"Frankly, I just noticed that he failed to register. He has left without paying his bill."

The Search · *12*

3   The Oasis

THOUGH MY STAY IN GHARDAÏA WAS MADE UNPLEASANT BY THE offensive character at the hotel, it is a fascinating place, a typical oasis: the largest of the seven cities of the region known as the Mzab. Its inhabitants, the Mozabites, Berbers of the Abadhite faith, are Moslem puritans who permit no deviation from the literal interpretation of the Koran. Originally driven south by the invading Arabs in the eleventh century, they sought refuge in an area so desolate that its very dread and isolation promised safety from further attack.

The name, Ghardaïa, is derived from a legend connected with the founding of the city. It is said that two Moslem saints, conversing in the desert, repeatedly noticed a light on a nearby hill. The disciple who was sent by one of the saints to investigate this phenomenon reported that he had found, in a cave, an abandoned young girl called Daia who was about to give birth to a child. Obligingly, the saint took her as his wife and planned a city around the cave. Thus, Ghar el Daia (Daia's Cave) is venerated to this day by Mozabite women, who burn candles and rub henna and perfume into the rock in memory of their brave sister.

The men are noted for their shrewd business sense and can be found as traders all over northern Africa, but no matter how far afield their affairs may take them, they always return to their homeland in the end. The town has a population of about fifteen thousand, including a minority of Arabs, Negroes and Jews.

From the arcades of the market place, the jumbled houses and a labyrinth of narrow streets rise to the exclusive area around the mosque with its leaning minaret. The houses have hardly any openings toward the street, and the door keys are so large that they can be used effectively as weapons. The market place is rich in local color, deliriously so at times. The most striking features of Ghardaïa are the countless wells and the lush date groves in the valley of the usually dry river Mzab.

When I met the colonel at the hotel, I told him about my experience.

"Rotten shame," he said. "Look here, why don't you come along with me as far as Tamanrasset? I already have a passenger, but I am sure we can squeeze you in. I am waiting for the fellow now. Odd sort of a chap . . . beard and all that sort of thing. . . . Hallo, here he comes. . . . Doesn't seem to be in a hurry. . . . My lorry is just around the corner. Don't know if we'll make it, but if you are ready to go. . . ."

I only had to pick up my duffel bag.

"Righto," said the colonel, "let's get cracking."

The hairline of a road through the central Sahara—a pronounced "washboard" at best, a dim track where it leads across volcanic plains or through the soft and treacherous sand—is repeatedly marked on the map as *très difficile*. A bond has to be posted by individual drivers in case a rescue party has to be sent out following a breakdown; night driving is forbidden (because people get lost more easily in the dark), and the French authorities have to be notified of arrivals and departures at each military post. During the hottest months of the year, from the middle of May until October, all traffic is suspended.

The colonel and I got off to a good start. We reached the oasis of El-Goléa the next day, but the rough road and the rocks of the black Tademaït plateau south of El-Goléa were very hard on the car. The colonel's other passenger, a young Frenchman, had an uncanny faculty for getting in the way and for saying the wrong thing. However, we all concurred on one point: we were glad to leave the Tademaït behind as we entered the region of smooth sand north of In-Salah. The colonel had barely ventured to remark: "I say, I think it's getting a bit better!" when we had a blowout. The Frenchman had so much to say about this that the colonel, struggling as he was with the spare tire, got exasperated.

"*Monsieur*," he said in his Oxford French, "you are always making conversation!"

The irony of this remark only became fully apparent later when his voluble passenger let it be known that he was going to the Hoggar for a period of religious meditation.

In-Salah was hot and exotic—smothered by dunes whose crests had been planted with hedges of palm fronds in an effort to keep drifting sand from invading the town. Many outlying houses were buried, and tall palms barely held their crowns above the dunes. The deep-green palm groves, the red houses with crenelated walls and raffia awnings, archways going nowhere in particular, camels dozing in vague stretches of sand, and a very native market made it quite close to a movie version of an oasis.

Because of the intense evaporation during the day, date plantations are irrigated by night. The distribution of the water is governed by old and very strict rules, and it is safe to say that more murders have been committed over disputes arising from the rationing of water than over affairs of the heart.

The harvest is threefold: dates are the main crop, but under the palms, fruit trees yield figs, peaches and apricots, and under the fruit trees, vegetables and melons are grown. About one hundred thousand tons of dates are consumed annually in the Sahara; another fifteen thousand tons are exported. The palm tree itself is of first importance in the native economy: the trunk is used for beams and doors in the construction of houses; cord, mats and bags are made from the fiber; the fronds are used for temporary shelters; the sap yields palm wine (*lagmi*); the pulp makes a fine hairdressing, and the date stones are collected for camel fodder.

How did the oases get started?

The earliest ones probably are contemporaneous with the appearance of the camel on the African continent. Some of the northern groups, founded by Berbers and Jews, date back to the sixth and seventh centuries. The penetration into the south took hundreds of years, so that settlements such as In-Salah (*Aïn Salah*: Good Well) are of much more recent origin. The oases of the northwestern Sahara are closely linked together and form a chain, an "avenue of palms," as the Arabs say. In the eastern Sahara oases are few and very far between. There are none in the central desert south of

In-Salah. There are only names of localities, such as Tiguel-guemine, Tiratimin, Amsir, until the traveler reaches Arak: one house, one European, and a lot of flies. Then, through mountains that once were the focal point of a volcanic explosion, the trail leads down to a wide plain and into the military post of Tamanrasset.

Here, after five days on the road together, the colonel, the Frenchman and I parted company.

TWO

THE BLUE MEN

1 *Hoggar*

A HUNDRED YEARS AGO A RENEGADE MEMBER OF THE HOGGAR
tribe, who had expatriated himself among the Arabs, said:
"If you accept a Targui's* hospitality, you have nothing to
fear from him under his tent or after you have left, but he
will notify his friends who will kill you and divide your
possessions."

Yet a military man, the gracious General Daumas, was
convinced in 1853 that, "If you are under the protection of

* Singular of Tuareg.

one, you will be safeguarded by all. You will be admirably received. You will suffer no want: the Targui will go hungry but offer you food, he will not drink but give you water, he will risk his life to save yours."

My sojourn among the Tuareg, those "vultures of the desert," was marred only by administrative suspicion and red tape. My only moments of discomfort were occasioned by a zealous little French lieutenant in Tamanrasset, where a slimy native policeman had been assigned to tail me day and night, armed with a four-foot whip. I was glad to get away from this outpost of civilization, and happy to find that the Tuareg were not afraid of me.

Ethnologically, the Tuareg are classified as "a Berber people"—among many other conjectures. Eminent authorities on the Sahara, notably Professor E. F. Gautier, believe them to be not merely a remnant but the ancestors of the ancient Egyptians, and the direct descendants of the Garamantes, a civilized Saharan people of the Fezzan, whose name has been perpetuated in the city of Djerma, the "Garama" of the Romans. Arab scholars believe the Tuareg to be Phoenicians. A French novelist stretched the puzzle of their origin to the point of portraying them as the survivors of Atlantis. They speak a language called Tamachec and use the only known Berber script: Tifinar, which can be written equally well from left to right, right to left, up or down. Socially, they are divided into three classes: nobles, vassals and Sudanese slaves, the present Harratin. Each tribe is headed by a chief (Amrar), the confederation by a sovereign (Amenokal). They are a pastoral, stock-raising

The Blue Men · 22

people. Their wealth lies in their herds of camels and goats. At harvest time the nobles everywhere break camp to move closer to the sparse agricultural centers, where the Harratin grow wheat and sorghum, to claim their share. In their role as incorruptible nomads, the Tuareg nobles hold that "shame enters with the plow." They know in advance that they will be cheated. The Harratin, on the other hand, are clever enough never to abuse the arrogance of their masters and only cheat up to a certain point. This astute balance of respect and tolerance is the basis of a happy relationship. There is not the slightest sign of oppression on the part of the masters, and no indication of servility in the behavior of the Harratin.

Originally, their economy was based on plunder. They bitterly resented the French conquest of the Sahara, knowing that it would put an end to the chief occupation of their lives: the safeguarding or raiding (as the case might be) of caravans that crossed their undisputed territory. Sporadically, the Tuareg struck back during the occupation of their realm long after the major battles had been won by the conqueror. Between the oases of El-Goléa and In-Salah, on the northern edge of the Tademaït plateau, the French had established a stronghold in the nineties called Fort Miribel. The country to the north had been "pacified" and the flat, waterless waste of black shale that stretched southward for two hundred and fifty miles seemed to render the place impregnable. The colonial troops considered it the worst punishment to be sent to this hellhole, where fits of madness were the order of the day. When, in 1916, the last garrison no longer gave any sign of life, a detachment of soldiers stationed at El-Goléa went south to investigate. They found the commander and his men in their bunks with their throats cut. A band of Tuareg had come unseen across the Tademaït and had silently murdered the defenders of the fort in their sleep. The inner walls of the men's quarters still show the dark stains of blood that splashed up to the ceiling.

When the Senousi drove the Italians out of the Fezzan during the first World War, a large stock of arms and ammunition fell into the hands of the natives. A chief of the Ikazkazan Tuareg of Aïr, Kaossen, who had been exiled by the French, acquired several machine guns and one cannon and organized a band of three hundred warriors. After defeating the military escort which had accompanied the Bilma salt caravan to Agades, he occupied the city and held the fort in check for four months. Although he had the sympathy of the sultan of Agades, his attitude toward the neighboring tribes was so despotic that he lost their support. He fled in 1918, greatly outnumbered by the troops that were sent against him. Some of the Tuareg tribes of Aïr did not submit to the military authorities until 1943.

The men's practice of hiding their faces, a unique custom, never has been satisfactorily explained. Some believe it to be a safeguard to prevent evil spirits from entering the body through the nose and mouth, others say that it is a protection against dust. They keep their faces hidden day and night, lifting the veil from below only when eating or drinking. The women, contrary to Moslem convention, go unveiled and enjoy absolute freedom until they decide to get married. The Tuareg abhor chickens and eggs and consider manual labor the lowest form of human degradation.

They are nominally Moslem, but their lives are almost entirely guided by superstitious beliefs and their faith in numerous amulets, worn on head, arms, legs and chest to ward off every imaginable evil.

The Arabs, in mortal fear of them, dubbed the Tuareg the "Abandoned of God"; they call themselves the "People of the Veil." They roam over an area of approximately one million five hundred thousand square miles throughout the southern Sahara and parts of the French Sudan. The movements of the various tribes are dictated by the need of pasture for their camels and goats. Since it does not rain for years on end, they migrate over enormous distances in the times of severe drought. Today they show a supreme indifference toward their conquerors, and their contempt for the Arabs has been extended to include airplanes and automobiles. For a long time they frowned upon the use of firearms because of the undignified noise they made and because it seemed cowardly to kill at a distance. They have few children, thanks to highly effective contraceptive methods held in secret by the women (one of three operations being the use of a substance similar to alum). Their songs are devoted to war, camels, and love.

In 1902, Tuareg resistance was broken in the Hoggar. A poem by one of the participants, preserved by Charles de Foucauld, the Saharan missionary who was murdered in Tamanrasset, is a pathetic final note to their defeat:

This I can tell you, fair women
And all of you who wear blue over mouth and nostrils:
Amessa was the scene of a violent combat

With lances, the guns of the pagans, and unsheathed swords.
I advanced toward the enemy, I struck and was struck
Until blood covered my shoulders and arms like a blanket.
The young women who play the violins will not be told
That I hid among the rocks,
For it is not true that, having fallen three times,
I was lifted up three times and carried away, unconscious,
Tied to a camel with ropes?
Because of this:
Defeat is not dishonour.
Long ago the pagans were victorious over the Prophet himself.

The Tuareg came to the conclusion that one of the rules of survival is to "kiss the hand you cannot sever." But the French plan "to transform into workers these eternal and useless vagabonds" has not succeeded. The only suitable job for them within the framework of the military administration is that of *méharistes,* members of the mounted desert police. Enlistment in the French Camel Corps is on a voluntary basis, and the terms are remarkably fair and flexible. Volunteers retain their native dress and may cancel their enlistment at any time for valid reason, the administration similarly reserving the right to dismiss any man should his services no longer be required. If qualified, they receive a monthly salary and may draw an advance payment to help them furnish their camels and personal equipment. The army provides the arms and ammunition. The *méharistes* are responsible for their provisions and the upkeep of their mounts. Funds for the replacement of camels are available only if loss or injury occur in the course of a military action.

2   *People of the Tents*

MY FIRST CONTACT WITH THE TUAREG HAD BEEN WITH A YOUNG noble who spoke excellent French. He was leaning against the counter of one of the tiny native stores in Tamanrasset, the military administration center of the Hoggar, idly studying the labels on the marmalade jars. A beautiful *takouba,* the long straight double-edged sword of the Tuareg, dangled at his hip. As I entered he adjusted his veil and turned to me with languid elegance to extend his slim hand, placing his palm against mine without pressing it and withdrawing it abruptly in the conventional greeting of his people. The upshot of the ensuing conversation was that he asked me: "You ride camel?"

"Yes," I said, "I would like to ride camel."

"Tomorrow morning, six o'clock. My name is Bahh. You get some tea and sugar and macaroni. Then you go with me to our encampments and to our pastures."

This was the chance for which I had been waiting.

At the appointed time next day Bahh's camels lay ruminating in the dry river bed: Erraït, the Strong One, and Abberim, Not Much White. They bared their teeth and produced a great variety of gurgling sounds while the *rahlas* were placed in front of the hump and the cinch was passed through the natural crevice under the chest.

Bahh pinched his camel's nose with his left hand jerking the head sideways, stepped in the crook of the neck with his left foot and swung his right leg over the saddle as the animal heaved upward, all in less time than it takes to tell.

"*Cravache!*" he called out.

I laid the whip on Erraït's rump to fall in step behind Not Much White. Our immediate objective was a camp two days' ride away where Bahh had to see a man about a camel.

Soon after reaching the far side of the river of sand we started to climb into a range of rock-strewn hills. Bahh began to sing a slow nasal tune with a rising hum at the end of each phrase. Camels, it is said, are very fond of music, and Bahh was rapidly becoming very fond of the aluminum water bottle I carried with me. By the time we stopped to rest he couldn't take his eyes off it. He sat fondling the smooth round sides and opening and closing the screw-on cap. He made it clear that he needed a canteen in the worst way. Nothing of the sort could be had for hundreds of miles around and, the water being what it was, I firmly intended to drink only my own, generously disinfected with Halazon tablets. I promised to give it to him before I returned to the coast.

"It would be nice for butter," said Bahh.

He cast covetous glances at the water bottle all that afternoon and his singing became peculiarly wistful. The next day he called my attention to the fact that the liquid goat butter had leaked copiously from his ordinary oil can down his camel's flank. This timely coincidence broke my heart. I gave him the bottle and watched him toss out my safe water to replace it eagerly with what was left of his rancid butter.

"Plenty of water in the *guerba*," he said. Yes, but I could hardly risk arousing his suspicion by slipping mysterious pills into our common goatskin water bag. From then on I had to rely on my injections and close my eyes to such visible hazards as manure, drowned insects and camel's hair.

While our own needs were small, a large supply of tea and sugar was a necessary cargo for distribution among natives who offered us their hospitality. The macaroni, properly seasoned and cooked with dried tomatoes, made an excellent soup called *sherba*.

The glare and the crushing heat of the day were drastically relieved by cold nights; the temperature easily dropped fifty degrees between sundown and early morning. I was a little dubious at first about sleeping on the ground, for wherever there is water, scorpions and horned vipers abound; but Bahh curled up with such complete confidence that I soon stopped worrying. No Targui ever suffered from insomnia or any other kind of subconscious insecurity.

When we approached the first encampment Bahh shed his white traveling robe and draped himself carefully in his purple *tahra,* a cotton material imported from India which has the quality of carbon paper and stains at the slightest touch. Since the Tuareg never bathe and believe that washing makes them ill, they acquire a dark blue sheen from head to foot that is considered very beautiful. Hence they are known as the Blue Men. The dryness of the desert, the wind and the loose garments effectively counteract their lack of sanitation.

"*Ourrt!*" called out Bahh. "*Ourrt!*"

Our camels lunged forward in a long trot and I could tell by the sharp leering eyes above the veil that I was being put to a test. The sense of balance I had acquired through past experience with horses was standing me in good stead.

Presently the encampment came into full view. A group of men walked slowly toward us wearing the customary *naïls*: sandals extending two inches around the foot to facilitate walking in loose sand. We couched our camels and exchanged greetings over and over again: *Labess,* No Evil, and *Hamdullah,* Praise to God.

They were nobles of the Kel Rela tribe who now conducted us to a tent presided over by a lady of refined features and great dignity: the perfect example of a matriarch. After inviting me to be seated on the rug the men slipped off their sandals and entered the tent to start within our circle a small fire of roots for the preparation of tea. The tent was clean and airy. There were saddles and leather traveling bags; swords, guns and daggers hung from the supporting posts. There was no shouting, no confusion, and no one asked me how I happened to be there, where I had come from or where I was going. As far as I could follow it the conversation was about my water (now butter) bottle which passed from hand to hand amidst the undivided admiration of those present. Bahh had stepped out of the tent. He returned carrying a handsome Sudanese bowl and carved spoon.

"This is for you," he said. "Come, I show you something."

In a depression a short distance away from camp some of the tribesmen had thrown a male camel on its side. The

The Blue Men · *30*

forefeet were hobbled, the hindfeet tied and stretched out by a man pulling at the other end of the rope. One native lay on the animal's belly, another on its neck, a third held down the snarling head. It looked like the capture of a prehistoric monster. One of the veiled men drew his dagger and proceeded to operate, deftly timing each stroke of the knife to the short intervals between the animal's convulsions. Red to the elbows, deaf to the hoarse groans of agony, he calmly carved away the bleeding organs and plunged his hand into the livid flesh to extricate the spermatic cord. Not a word was spoken among the men; only Bahh turned to me in explanation.

"Amahli is very hard to handle. We make him *indhá*."

A handful of sand was thrown on the wound and the animal untied and allowed to kneel. Then Bahh put his saddle in place, mounted, and the howling white camel strode into the sunset, its hindquarters covered with running blood.

The Tuareg eat when they are hungry, at any time it pleases them: in the afternoon, in the evening, or at two o'clock in the morning. The thud-thud of the women pounding sorghum had been going on all the while. A fire was blazing under a large pot outside of a nearby tent.

My rudimentary knowledge of the language was a barrier to close understanding, to be sure, but their ability at once to comprehend an inference of gesture or expression helped substantially to overcome this handicap. My eagerness to learn a few essential phrases of Tamachec pleased them, and my use of it made their hard eyes melt with laughter. One of the men began to tap on an upturned brass receptacle. There were yelps of gaiety when I joined them in the sharply punctuated chant. Silently, gracefully, visitors came and went, the kind of people who never jostle each other, never step on one's feet in a crowd.

Like everyone in the Sahara I wore baggy trousers, tied at the ankles. I also had a five-yard length of cotton material for a headcloth, called *shesh*. My friends now insisted that I wear it in their fashion, covering the lower part of the face to the bridge of the nose, loosely flowing around the neck, and tightly wound around the head down to the eyebrows. They watched me closely as I tied the cloth, approved, and continued to sing. Suddenly, a few minutes later, they stopped, remained silent, then leveled imaginary guns at me. They mimicked shots and indicated that I had to leave the tent. I staggered around in the darkness outside, a trifle bewildered, while the singing and tapping resumed. Finally one of the men called and waved me back. They looked at me sharply as I re-entered the tent. Following their example I, too, lowered my veil, whereupon they all fell over on their sides with laughter.

They absolutely refused to tell me what it was all about. Some sort of a game, some sort of a test.

Later, a Negro brought two steaming bowls of food, cereal in the one and great hunks of meat in the other. We each took one of the wooden spoons from the top of the cereal bowl, swallowed a mouthful, and stuck the spoon back with the handle pointing out.

"Dig deeper!" my neighbor urged me, handing me a choice piece of mutton. Most of the cherished rancid butter had sunk to the bottom of the bowl. The meat was tender and delicious, its flavor in no way impaired by the liberal dose of sand which is a standard adjunct to desert cuisine.

When we had finished I decided to perform what I had hoped would be recognized as another example of white man's magic. I had brought with me several packages of pudding powder which requires no cooking. Knowing how fond the Tuareg are of sweets I felt convinced that this would meet with their approval. I confidently measured out two cups of goat's milk, stirred the powder into it, tasted the delightful mixture and handed it to my host. He politely dipped the tip of his spoon into it and licked it stoically, pronounced judgment with a word I didn't understand but which, unmistakably, meant thumbs down, for all the rest of them declined. They were afraid of magic, even sweet. My experiment had failed. At this critical moment Bahh returned. It was eleven-thirty. He had ridden the freshly castrated camel steadily for four hours. He said it was fine.

Near our tent a space had been cleared of loose rock and the ground neatly smoothed within a square bounded on three sides by sturdy leather-edged mats. My saddle and traveling kit stood in one corner, my sleeping bag had been unrolled. Someone had prepared my shelter for the night.

The next day I noticed that the Negro servant had salvaged the wrapper of the pudding powder. He had carefully divided it and wore the two printed sides as decorations in his turban, from which they stuck out like little wings.

3   Manners and Camels

LAZY AS THEY ARE, THE TUAREG OF THE HOGGAR KEEP THEIR
tents in good order and free from the nauseating odors and
unsanitary conditions prevailing in most of the Saharan
hotels. For all the ever-changing camps and passing caravans
a traveler can ride for weeks across the desert without seeing
any trash or refuse. The natives urinate kneeling and always
cover up their tracks. Only death leaves its wreckage in the
sand.

When receiving a visitor the master of a tent is expected to
take three steps forward. In the dark, when it is impossible
to recognize even a friend who is completely wrapped in
blue, a Targui will offer his greeting and obligingly mention his name. Like their parents, the children speak in soft
undertones. They are generally very good-looking, but it is
a serious breach of etiquette to say so outright, for to call
someone's child beautiful is tantamount to giving it the evil
eye. The safe way to pay such a compliment is to say that
the child is pleasing. In courting one of the lithe and comely
girls the approach is even more indirect. The proper time for
it is during an *ahal,* a musical and literary gathering. Flirt-
ing is not done face to face. A young man gradually closes
in on the lady of his choice until he finds the moment
propitious to sit behind her. During the next hour or so he
patiently waits for a sign of encouragement. Should none

be forthcoming, he simply moves away again, but if the lady is well-disposed, he may whisper in her ear that his camel is couched near a certain thornbush. If this announcement has the desired effect, the girl will literally lean over backward and permit her lover to inhale the breath of her nostrils, and if she is inclined to go beyond this voluptuous introduction, she may then and there whisper back to him that she would like to park her camel next to his. Under the thornbush, of course, the subterfuge ends.

The Tuareg are monogamous, but they usually have a number of concubines in various encampments and among the Harratin. In this connection, a child born to a Tuareg woman by a foreigner automatically becomes a member of the woman's tribe, whereas the offspring of a Targui and a non-Tuareg woman does not. They say: "It is the womb that marks the child." Still, Tuareg mothers are quite unsentimental. Until, and for some time after, the French conquest, infanticide was widely practiced. Among the aristocracy of certain tribes, young girls of exceptional promise are forced to drink from eight to twelve quarts of goats' or camels' milk a day. As a result of this artificial fattening the chosen few weigh around three hundred pounds by the time they reach the age of eighteen or twenty. Excessive obesity, in a country where everyone tends to be lean, is much admired, as are husbands who can afford wives whose every move requires the help of three or four strong men.

Despite his idiosyncrasies, blessed with a marvelous capacity for repose and entirely free from our adulation of facts and figures, the Targui has achieved a thoroughly

Manners and Camels · 35

integrated way of life in marked contrast to our own, which is to such a large extent a series of expediencies and maladjustments. In our cities people tear through breakfast, hurry to the office, rush to an appointment as if business *cum* jangling telephones were more important than life itself. In the evening, too rattled for sex, they escape from themselves amidst the unrealities of a movie or television. They erect skyscrapers and stuff them full of antiques, build enormous factories to manufacture "home-made" bread. Radio and jukebox crooners drool over unrequited love. Even news reports seem slanted to keep the public jittery and anxious for the next installment of disaster. The common retort to this is that ours is a much more complex civilization, but if we wear ourselves to a frazzle with complications and inanities this very complexity must be a mistake.

In giving information the Tuareg are reliable and precise, not about the exact distance in miles but the time it will require to reach a certain point. This is perfectly reasonable, for ten miles may present more obstacles than fifty. For practical purposes knowledge of the distance is worthless, whereas an estimate in time covers all existing conditions. A native will look at you and your mount, add to it the nature of the terrain and, taking into consideration attendant circumstances such as weather and the time of day or night, tell you exactly how long it will take you to reach your destination.

If a traveler should get lost, his best guide to immediate safety, the nearest waterhole, would be his camel. Provided there is any water within a radius of twenty miles, a camel is bound to find its way to it. Many men have gone mad in the desert, plagued by hallucinations of sparkling lakes and shady groves. No camel has ever been fooled by a mirage.

But many people are fooled by camels. For instance, the rumor that camels copulate back to back is false. It probably got started (with Pliny!) because, in a lax condition, the males' penis points to the rear. This peculiarity is modified by erection. Actually, the male approaches a couched female from behind, spreads his forelegs over her back with his neck next to hers, and maneuvers his hindquarters into an appropriate crouching position. Perhaps the misconception has persisted for so long because camels very rarely make love in the presence of man.

They hate to be separated from their own group and are as conventional as cats in their habits once they get used to a routine. They will lie down in exactly the same place as they have on previous occasions, and pack camels will make a great fuss if they are not placed in their habitual order in the caravan file.

In spite of its renowned endurance and sobriety an active camel cannot go without water longer than five days during the hot season. Pasturing in ideal circumstances it can stretch days into weeks and even months. A creature born in solitude and accustomed to lean pickings, full of contradictions, extremely sensitive, profoundly misunderstood, it has what is known as "the artistic temperament." The camel is docile and obedient in a contemptuous sort of way, patient and resigned, but when least expected it will flare up at a minor

Manners and Camels • *37*

provocation or for no apparent reason at all in violent and disproportionate revolt. At such moments it can be obstreperous to the point of suicide. It will stop in its tracks and no dagger jabs will budge it; it will kneel and rather die than rise again, even if a fire is kindled under it. It will freeze into immobility over a shadow, it will have a fit over a wrinkle in the saddle blanket, but if it steps on a six-inch thorn it will merely stamp its foot until the obstruction is driven in, and keep on walking. When the sole of one of the pads has worn through it is an accepted practice for the Tuareg to stitch on anything that is handy. By the time the patch is gone, the foot has very likely healed. More than anything the camel hates sharp rocks and wet ground. It does not seem to mind the heat but has a very low resistance to humidity. It will turn up its nose at lush green pastures and savor shrubs that have the properties of steel wool. Left to browse in peace, the animal ambles from clump to clump selecting tiny mouthfuls. Then it lies down to digest this prickly entanglement, staring into the distance. It can drink twenty-five gallons of water at one time but perspires very little. Its skin is twice as thick as cowhide.

There are two distinct types of camels: the pack animal of the caravans, the coarse *djemel,* and the fleet and elegant *méhari,* or riding camel.

The nomads practice selective breeding and there are many definite strains. A good *méhari* has a full hump and firm lips; a deep chest; legs well muscled to the knees and lean from there on down to ensure a fast and easy gait; a broad head tapering to a narrow muzzle; large eyes with heavy lids and long, dense lashes for protection against sun and sand.

Usually one male is kept to service from fifty to a hundred females. The cows are coy and restless during the rutting season, the bulls extremely fierce. They are intensely jealous of any male that dares to cut in on their harem and will readily launch a merciless fight, each biting the other furiously about the neck and testicles, each trying to throw the other to crush and trample him to death. Often after such battles the female most in heat will kneel beside the victor, who promptly seeks solace in coitus.

The period of gestation is twelve months, the weight and volume of the newborn calf equivalent to that of a full-grown man. It can stand up and totter about after a week and soon makes friends with other calves, who form separate little cliques to play and investigate the steel-wool pastures.

A year later the calf has its right nostril pierced and the ring inserted to which the guiding rein will be attached. At the age of two it is branded, either with the tribal mark or that of individual ownership. Branding is a custom so ancient that its origin has been lost in the nebulous past of Oriental history. It was current in Arabia many centuries before the first invasion of North Africa. Later Arab conquests introduced it to Spain, and via the Spanish migration to North America it eventually became a practice among cattlemen of the Old West in recent years.

All working camels insist on taking six months off each year. They achieve this simply be refusing any load, or rider, after a certain number of trips, and make it plain that they wish to be left alone. During their vacations they wander far and wide in search of nourishment, but they never get lost in regions devoid of water.

The training of young camels takes much gentleness and patience, for if mishandled at an early age they may remain intractable forever. Teaching them to stay in one place is easy. The rein is simply tied to a foreleg; each time the camel moves there is a painfull pull on the nostril. Thus it soon learns to stand still with the rein dropped on the ground. To make it kneel is a little more difficult and takes two at first: the rider, who gives the proper signal, and a man on the ground who strikes the animal's knee at the same time until it learns to couch at the rider's command alone. But it is in teaching it to respond to guidance by pinching its neck with bare toes that the understanding trainer is rewarded in the end by the camel's instant obedience to signals to start, run, slow down, stop, turn, back or couch.

The widely accepted notion that riding a camel can cause seasickness is nonsense. It is true that, as a consequence of its characteristic single-foot gait, there is a slight swaying motion, but I never have known of anyone who has *really* become sick; I have only heard the falsehood repeated by people who never rode a camel. Except in the trot, that is, a fast pace, riding a camel is less fatiguing than riding a horse. For one thing, it does not demand the same constant attention. A horse's movements are quicker and his inclination to change direction arbitrarily is more pronounced. A camel, and especially a string of camels in a caravan, will follow a set course for hours. Unless frightened or forced to do so, the camel does not gallop.

It is fully grown at the age of fifteen, useful until it is

twenty-two, and would live to forty and fifty if it were not ordinarily butchered earlier. Not that a few years more or less make any difference in the quality of the meat. Camel is always tough. It has no particular flavor but a pungent odor of old wet leather.

4   The Harratin

SOME OF THE NOBLES IN BAHH'S ENCAMPMENT WERE PREPARING to visit a village of Harratin. While the camels were being saddled by their servants, they took out their "compacts" and painted their eyes. Using a thorn and starting from the inside corner of the eye, they dexterously applied the black *dazould,* a viscous powder made of ground stone, to the pink conjunctiva of the lid.

This accentuates the white of the eyeballs and makes the eyes appear exceedingly bright. It does not indicate that the Tuareg are sissies! Far from it. In deference to their paradoxical vanity be it said that the application of the cosmetic is also believed to prevent ophthalmia.

I asked Bahh, "Is the king of the Tuareg in this vicinity?"

He said, "Yes. He is at Emmekhenni."

"Where is Emmekhenni?"

He pointed south. "Over there."

"I would like to meet the king of the Tuareg. Do you think that is possible?"

Bahh didn't answer. Instead, he decided to get his head

shaved. He unwound the six yards of purple cloth that covered his face and head, a most unusual thing to do in the presence of a stranger and, in a sense, a subtle compliment to a visitor's discretion. A request to photograph him undisguised would have drawn instant refusal; an attempt to take a picture of him on the sly could have had serious consequences and barred me from any further association with his people. It was obviously his conviction that I would not embarrass him by such a *faux pas* that put him at his ease. He had a handsome, sensitive face, blue lips and dusky skin. Fazzi, a Sudanese, was in attendance as the barber. Dagger in hand, he cleared the cranium of all hair that had grown since the last treatment from the forehead back, leaving intact only a small patch of long hair with three meticulously braided pigtails. An amulet in a flat pouch remained untouched on the top of Bahh's head. When the job was done to his satisfaction he took the veil between his teeth and wound it across his face and about his head again, the end falling loosely over his shoulders.

The nobles invited me to join them and suggested that I take Fazzi along. Bahh strapped on his sword, hitched his saddle bags to the *rahla,* and took off alone, saying that he would catch up with us later. As he rode away he gave Fazzi some instructions in Tamachec.

During the noon hours we unsaddled and hobbled the camels, propped up swords and rifles in the *rahlas* and tied blankets over the structure as a temporary shelter from the blazing sun. Fazzi, magnificent in his shabby turquoise rags, started a fire, unpacked the tea things and set about preparing *kesra,* the bread of the Tuareg. Mixing the coarse flour with the muddy water from the goatskin, he shaped the dough into a flat cake two inches thick. This he placed directly on the coals. The underside cooked to a firm consistency, the soft upper surface absorbed every grain of blowing sand. Then he turned the cake over. Retrieving it from the fire, he rinsed it off casually, scraped the black crust of coals from both sides, broke it in pieces and placed it before us in a wooden bowl. It was very good, dipped in liquid goat butter.

As we traveled in a southwesterly direction the character of the country began to change. Here, volcanoes had boiled over and spewed forth a mass of granite from the bowels of the earth. Sandy depressions gave way to regions of pierced and hollowed boulders of incredible dimensions that looked as if a giant Henry Moore had fashioned them in a creative frenzy over a period of a thousand years. It was hard to believe that nature, by sheer accident, could produce monuments so distinctly sculptural. Here and there enormous heaps of rock suggested the effort of a mighty helper who had tried to put this chaotic workshop in order. It was all a little out of focus in the heat; only things at close range persisted in exaggerated sharpness: the dense carpet of flies on the shady side of every rider, the bright blue lizards standing bowlegged on the black rocks.

When we were once more on open ground a group of riders approached, right hand held up Indian fashion in friendly greeting; a Dagh Rahli noble and his retainers. Swathed from head to foot in indigo and mounted on a superb white *méhari,* he sidled up to our camels to rub palms with us. After countless mutual assurances that there was indeed No Evil, Praise to God, he was about to dismount when his camel started to act up. The close proximity of the females we were riding was too much for his fine *khimbar*, a breed famous for its beauty, endowed with blue eyes and three perfectly matched fur buttons evenly spaced in a row on the ridge of the nose. A bubble-shaped mucous membrane, the size of a large fist, which issues from the mouth of male camels during the mating season, hung quivering from the left side of the animal's lips. Roaring defiantly when the Dagh Rahli reached forward to grab its nose, rumbling inside, foaming at the mouth and shedding water, the frustrated beast whirled and plunged about and wildly stamped its feet while the strong neck writhed and twisted like a tortured snake. Enveloped in a thick cloud of dust, his garments billowing, the rider managed to keep his seat, but our camels were alarmed. With the greatest difficulty the frantic *khimbar* was brought sufficiently under control by his master to be headed off in the right direction. The rest of the cortege followed solemnly, including two Negroes, perched on the very rear ends of their donkeys, who were driving a few broadtail sheep. Fazzi looked at the sheep admiringly and remarked with the voice of the connoisseur: *"Il y'en a de la graisse bien ça le mouton beaucoup!"* or "There's a lot of fat on those sheep all right!"

On waking in the morning we would often find that two or three tribesmen had joined our company during the night. They were never heard or seen when they arrived. Usually they had come from a place that was identified by no more than a legend, and were bound for a destination obscurely related to a past event. A peculiar methodical aimlessness governed their wanderings and spurred them on in the four directions of the compass along a network of invisible trails of which the cardinal points were the waterholes. They barely opened their mouths, but in an atmosphere of perfect harmony they would share our tea or bid us to their fire, pack their camels unhurriedly and ride away.

At last the monotony of volcanic devastation was relieved by a strip of vegetation as we came within sight of the settlement of Harratin. Some of the Negroes stepped out of their *zeribas* (round huts made of long, tough grass) to await our arrival. One fellow with a winning grin invited us into his miniature patio, an enclosure that extended in a semicircle around the entrance to the hut. Here we left our saddles and other equipment and, with many mutual affirmations that evil had been banished from the earth and everyone was in the best of health, presented a good measure of sugar and tea. The women were shy and discreetly curious. Tiny as it was, the hut was divided by a grass partition into "parlor" and bedroom. One of the women brought a pathetic little rug for me to sit on, and our host, still grinning, scooped a hole out of the sand in the middle of the floor to lay a fire. Fazzi, playing man-of-the-world, made a deep impression speaking French to me and interpreting with so many embellishments that everyone was spellbound. To the Harratin all foreigners were Swiss, because the year before a gentleman from Zurich had stopped among them to recuperate from exposure. He had left as a gift an elegant wrist watch, which now only ticked for a few seconds when knocked against a rock or someone's head.

"The Swiss," explained Fazzi, "he was always thirsty. The heat, she was too much for him. The face, he was very red. The feet, he was swollen like this, all blisters. Camels, he never want to see them again. The Mirican [American], he can take it, *gyddygyd*."

Our circle was widening as more of the Harratin quietly slipped into the hut. After the tea a large bowl of goat meat and cereal was served. Then our host brought out his bamboo flute to play what sounded like the introduction to a fugue. To revive the fire he reached behind from time to time to pluck a handful of the dry blades of grass from the wall of the hut. In the middle of the musicale one of the black women, holding a baby in her arms, peeked through the break in the partition. Upon seeing the white bogeyman the baby shrieked in uncontrollable fright. The mother patted her child affectionately on the behind and retreated with a wry smile. When the party broke up, Fazzi went to sleep in the enclosure outside. I had been given the run of the place, so to speak. The fire still glimmered in the hollow of sand and the only sound till morning was the staccato bark of a jackal.

Our points of repair were never anything that had concrete meaning, never anything that was marked on a map. There were scenes of ribbed spires and phallic cones, shapely dunes floating in mid-air far off in another dimension, black slabs of rock spreading fanwise out of the ground. There were nightmares solidified in lava, monstrous panoramas of all the symbols of obscenity, and always, intermittently, broad troughs of sand.

On the level stretches we jogged along at a fast pace. The exhilaration of the brisk movement invariably made Fazzi sing after the manner of warriors who ride in a "carousel," when the women play their single-stringed violins and the men trot their caparisoned camels around them in perfect rhythm to the music.

Leh hamiee-ne wan-i leh hamah
Leh hamiee-ne wan-i leh hamah....

It was just getting dark when we came upon a crowd of dancers swaying and weaving in a cloud of dust, the men on the inside, the women forming an outer circle. To the accompaniment of several flutes, half a dozen tom-toms beat in counter-rhythm to the booming of a much larger drum. With intricate steps the dancers moved forward and backward and intertwined, hesitated and turned with upheld arms. Occasionally the husky chanting was dominated by a single falsetto voice: "He has returned . . . he has returned. . . ." The graceful black women with buttered hair and bright yellow spots on their cheeks slithered about rolling their hips. They wore large silver loops in their ears and their braids were bound with copper wire and studded with shining ornaments. At intervals the men took a few puffs from slender pipes that had three brass rings hanging from the bottom of the bowl. Hour after hour the sound and the movement flowed on in a smooth and beguiling hashish trance, the dust and the darkness soon hiding all

The Harratin • 47

but the gleam of white teeth or the faint flash of a jewel. The high-pitched solo voices were answered by the chorus: "He has returned . . . he has returned . . ." Who? Whence? They didn't say and it didn't matter. It was incentive enough to make them sing and dance. The phrase was repeated again and again, yet the chant never lagged; it expressed so many fine shades of joy. The musicians who produced this spell were inversely so affected by it that they, in turn, became the instruments of a compelling force which acted upon them like a powerful intoxicant and urged them on to ever more ethereal modulations and wilder frenzy, while the dancers responded ecstatically, imbued as they were with the pleasant event, absorbed in the complicated rhythm. They themselves were joy and rhythm, the physical projection of a happy thought, the consummation of a rapture that thrived on their sensuous energy until it finally drifted away into the night along with the dust and the acrid smoke of *kif*.

The next day the desert was silent again and it was hard to believe that it could ever beget anything other than a hot and hostile inertia.

5   *King of the Tuareg*

WE WERE SITTING IN THE MIDDLE OF A DRY WASH, BOILING water for tea. Fazzi heaved a stone at the nearest thornbush to drive away the evil spirits who lurk in such places to vex the traveler.

"The mint," he said, "we have him no more."

Upon seeing my disappointment he looked around and, after examining the sparse vegetation, picked a handful of minute gray stalks. He crushed them in his hand and dropped the brittle fragments into the pot. The wonderfully aromatic plant, called *dinharh,* had an exquisite flavor and proved once again the constant contradiction of indigence and refinement so characteristic of the nomad. Nor was this the only contradiction. The Tuareg carried all their possessions in leather bags. Those containing valuables they would lock with their native *cadenas,* three keys sometimes being required to work the combination. The system seemed singularly ineffectual as a measure of precaution because every man carried a dagger and anyone who so desired could ignore the lock and slash the leather bag. But no one thought of doing this. The lock was universally respected as a symbol of privacy.

Without looking up, Fazzi announced: "You hear something? The people, they are coming right now, soon."

I couldn't hear or see a thing; nothing moved in the yellow emptiness.

"Two riders, over there."

Now I could barely recognize a feeble vapor rising from the ground to the south.

"Bahh and Marahli."

So it was; Bahh on a creamy-white *méhari* that had a tassel three feet long swinging from its right shoulder, Marahli on a splendid black mount. After the ritual of greeting Bahh stretched his blue legs and sang a muffled, quavering tune. In due time he revealed that he had been in the encampment of the supreme chief.

"The Amenokal," he said with a twinkle in his eye, "he wants to meet the polite stranger who can run a camel. He has put off breaking camp to receive you; three days' ride from here. Fazzi knows the way."

I told him how much I appreciated his speaking favorably of me, and that I was honored by the Amenokal's invitation. He smiled and implied with a grand gesture: the Sahara is yours. Marahli sat with black unblinking eyes, a moody and somnolent fellow with a coiled spring inside.

At dawn we parted company. The black and the white camel turned east, Fazzi and I climbed toward a jagged ridge in the opposite direction. Zigzagging and doubling back through rocks we came upon a waterhole fringed by palms and guarded by a swarm of fierce insects. A young black girl came dancing from behind a boulder with a string of donkeys to fetch water for an encampment, highly amused to find a white civilian on her beat. Fazzi had a hard time keeping up with her cooing and bubbling. I asked him to find out if she knew of any inscriptions or pictographs in the vicinity.

"Yes," he interpreted, "she says there are plenty, all over the rocks and on her belly, too."

We filled our goatskins and helped replenish hers. This so delighted her that, with a show of artful coquetry, she indicated how welcome we were to enjoy all she had to offer.

"The girl," said Fazzi, "if you don't want to make love to her, she would like you to give her something anyway."

"A cigarette, for instance?"

"*Gyddygyd.*"

I gave her three and she gaily waved us on our way.

Once, in a crowded city, a man bumped into me coming around a corner. He didn't apologize in the ordinary way. Before he hurried on, he stopped for a moment and said in dismay: "Ah, too many of us! Too many of us!"

Here, wind, sand and space merged into an absolute that could not be measured by the standards of our familiar world. There were so very few people at any given point at any certain time.

We traversed an area of dusty clumps of shrubbery. The Amenokal's camp lay ahead somewhere in the blue haze on the edge of infinity. It occurred to me the next morning that it might be in order to address the chief in Tamachec. I asked Fazzi: "What can I say to the Amenokal to please him when we arrive in his camp?"

"Anything you like," he said. "If you want to make him happy, you tell him: *Nak dewair salis hwadewa y djerarh addounedh hyieren houlan arrech abbadah idiss deedawah abbadah.*"

"Are you sure that is the thing to say?"

"Yes, he will be pleased *beaucoup*. You speak to him in Tamachec, I tell you what he says after that."

I became so engrossed in perfecting my pronunciation that I forgot to ask him about the meaning of the words, and then a number of tents appeared among the boulders at the foot of a hill.

"This is Emmekhenni," said Fazzi.

At high noon it was the center of a furnace. Nobody paid any attention to us as we unsaddled our camels. A few men stalked about as if they were walking in their sleep. Obviously, no one was going to acknowledge our presence before

King of the Tuareg • *51*

the chief did us the honor. A black girl brought a fine rug and spread it carefully on the sand. I felt more exposed on it than sitting on the ground, but Fazzi insisted that desert etiquette demanded such decorum. The sun was almost unbearable and the flies were so thick that only extreme fatalism could put up with them.

At last a group of dignitaries, the Amenokal in front, came walking down the hillside at a slow, studied pace. I stepped forward and we all rubbed palms. The chief bade me be seated again on the rug, where he joined me; his entourage of twenty nobles sat down in a row behind him in the sand. Dizzy as I was from the heat, the ordeal of being subjected to a severe scrutiny by a gimlet-eyed congregation of veiled men made me feel a bit queasy.

I had been told that, more than anything, Amenokal Baï disliked nervous, impatient, fidgety people; quick, restless gestures; unnecessary noise; and anyone who was stupid enough to be in a hurry. Like all his nobles he was superbly aristocratic; a large, portly man with tapering hands and eagle eyes, immaculate in an apricot-colored robe and white veil. He waited for me to open the session. Now was the time to say my piece in Tamachec.

It was received in dead silence. Somehow they seemed more dumbfounded than pleased; or perhaps they were not diposed to show their emotion. Their austerity nearly made me lose my composure.

"Fazzi," I said, "please tell the Amenokal that I sincerely appreciate his invitation and that I am very happy to be among the Tuareg."

This was met by a murmur of approval.

The Blue Men · *52*

A Negro deposited a wooden box near the rug and the chief's lieutenant made a fire and set glasses and pots about him in the sand. While we sipped the piping hot mint tea a bevy of black women filed past carrying poles, bales and rocks on their heads. A little way down the slope they started to put up a tent. Their slow, precise movements looked more like a ballet routine than hard work.

During this first encounter conversation was limited to an exchange of courtesies, one of which misfired due to Fazzi's interpreting.

"The Amenokal," he said, "he has the tent put up for you."

I expressed my admiration for it and was surprised that there was so much comment after Fazzi got through translating. I was aware that he was talking too much but couldn't understand what the hubbub was all about. Finally he stopped long enough to tell me: "The Amenokal, he says the tent is not for sale."

"For sale? I had no intention of buying it! What in hell did you tell him? Fazzi, I don't want you to make things up! I couldn't afford to buy it even if I wanted to, but don't mention that. Tell him that I meant to say how much I liked it—and don't cross me up again, *tu comprends?*"

This time he got it straight and my firm attitude must have appealed to the chief because something almost like a smile sparkled in his eyes for an instant. He rose, slipped on his sandals, and all the nobles got up to follow him. Fazzi and I moved into the tent.

"By the way," I said, "my speech fell rather flat. What, exactly, did it mean?"

"You tell him," said Fazzi brightly, *" 'Et moi, je suis content avec ça les types parce que j'y vois les types; et moi, quand je trouve, je marche avec toi tous les jours parce que j'ai gagné par le tête.' "* ("I am glad to be with you guys because I wanted to meet you guys; and me, when I find out where you are, I travel with you day after day because I am learning something every minute.")

His intentions were perfectly good; the trouble was with the way his mind worked. Coming from a distinguished visitor, a greeting phrased in the cocky familiarity of the underdog naturally brought a negative response from the Amenokal and his nobles. However, far from being offended, they understood my predicament and judged my behavior by the intrinsic respect I showed them. They undoubtedly felt that my visit was motivated by genuine interest. They derived very little profit from my presence and their confidence could not be bought with a few pounds of sugar and tea.

The tent was made of sixty goatskins, tanned a rich rust color and decorated with leather tassels. The main posts were carved around the top and stood about five and a half feet at the highest point. The sides sloped down in two graceful dips to lower supports and from there to the ground where the edges were lashed to rocks with leather thongs. It was open toward the east; two strong fiber mats extended at right angles from the entrance as windbreaks. The back flap could be let down or lifted up and thrown over the top to allow maximum ventilation. A heavy rug was spread inside.

Fazzi and I were left alone the rest of the day. It was

pleasant to relax in the shade, sheltered from the glare of the desert. Toward evening the Negro brought a large foaming bowl of camel's milk, fresh and sweet with a delicate almond flavor. There was never a harsh voice, never a bawling child; only once a minor commotion occurred outside when someone killed a horned viper that had lain hidden in the sand.

Next morning, in the crystal-clear air, hundreds upon hundreds of pure-bred camels with their little ones came swaying ponderously over a knoll on the edge of the encampment, raising a prodigious cloud of dust. When one of the calves strayed from the herd, its mother would break into a run with outstretched neck and bring it back to the fold, gurgling in maternal rebuke.

Amenokal Baï's second visit was less formal than the initial reception. This time he came as a friend. Ten of the nobles entered the tent with him. Fazzi brewed the tea. It so happened that my bedroll lay behind Baï and I could see that he was puzzled by it. I spread it out and gave a demonstration. This made a much better impression than the pudding powder. What fascinated him most was the zipper. Fazzi, the expert on foreign matters, answered all questions and put on a blasé air as if he had invented this miracle of convenience. Zippers were really a bit boring, you know, when you were surrounded by them every day. But the Amenokal didn't think so. He pulled the slide partway down the track, studied the effect, quickly pulled it up again, slowly pulled it down a little farther than before and back as fast as lightning to the starting point.

"Are there many of these?" he asked.

"Yes, in my country they are made in great quantities, like goatskin water bags in the Sahara."

Fazzi took about ten minutes to put this across, probably with sundry metaphysical explanations of all the goblins involved in the manufacture and operation of the mechanism and some skeptical remarks about its durability and ultimate worth. After all, so many trucks broke down, so many airplanes crashed; it was reasonable to assume that most zippers got stuck sooner or later.

The Amenokal was still interested enough to ask if it had come from far away. This was his prudent method of finding out where I had come from—since he could not be so crude as to ask me outright. It would also give him a clue to the geographical position of Zipperland.

"It comes from the interior of America," I said, "nearly ten thousand miles away, across a big sea."

They had vaguely heard of Mirica, but the distance made no sense to them.

I said: *"Maya! Maya!* Much, much water!"

They couldn't conceive of that much water.

Then I had an idea. I made a rough calculation.

"Fazzi," I said, "tell them that, if I had ridden a camel all the way, it would have taken me two hundred and eighty days to come here."

They were utterly amazed. Everybody talked at once.

With a mentality that constantly fluctuated between fancy and reality they did not differentiate between fact and hypothesis and made themselves believe that I had indeed performed the astounding feat of traveling the entire distance by camel. Two hundred and eighty days! It took only twenty days to Timbuctoo!

When the flurry had subsided the Amenokal asked searchingly: "Are there any Tuareg in Mirica?"

"No," I had to admit. The thought of veiled blue warriors on Fifth Avenue was a little disturbing.

I knew that Amenokal Baï had consistently refused to be photographed. To my surprise he not only consented to let me take his picture but showed me the courtesy of lowering his veil to the tip of his nose.

The symbol of his authority is the *tobol,* an enormous drum which can be heard within a radius of ten miles. Only the Amenokal in person can give the order to strike the *tobol.* It is sounded to summon the warriors.

No one was summoned when Fazzi and I departed after three days but, as we led our camels out of the camp, many of the nobles we had met walked along with us to wish us well on our return to Tamanrasset. One by one they rubbed palms with us before they went back to their tents. One of the Tuareg placed a fine silver ornament in my hand, another gave me a beautiful brass lock. The last to leave, a battle-scarred old warrior, presented me with an embroidered potholder as a parting gift.

THREE

AZALAÏ

1   *The Road to Gao*

THE SAHARA HAD NOT DISAPPOINTED ME. THE TRIP TO THE
Hoggar had helped me to get into my stride. The nomads
had accepted me and I felt thoroughly at home with them.
Unfortunately, my money ran out, as usual. I had to go back
to New York to get another job. But my experience with the
Tuareg tribesmen had been so revealing that, when the opportunity came after two intervening years, I set out for
Africa once more, this time with the express purpose of
joining a native camel caravan. I was convinced that, in the

Sahara, a way of life persists that dates back to Biblical times. This was very intriguing to me.

As a first step in my search for a caravan I took the train from Algiers to Colomb-Béchar, the northern terminal of the S.A.T.T. (*Société Africaine des Transports Tropicaux*), which operates a truck line across the Sahara.

There were photographs of Fontainebleau over the seats in the train compartment, and snatches of conversation in French and Arabic above the rattling of the windows. Ox teams were plowing the rich fields of the *mitidja,* the coastal plain, and Arabs in grandly flowing robes drove overladen donkeys along the country lanes. It took most of a day and a full night to get to Colomb-Béchar, a dreary trip, especially in the dark. The Hoggar road, which I had taken two years before, was closed.

As I traveled toward the desert again, I hoped that I wasn't stretching my luck too far in assuming that a hardened band of camel drivers would consent to take along a stranger on a caravan. Perhaps, even if they were willing, they wouldn't want to be saddled with the responsibility in case anything happened to him. Apart from that, I would have to get official permission from the authorities, and they might think that I was just another *fou illuminé,* a visionary fool who thought he had the world by the tail. The idea of an American wanting to cross the Sahara with a native caravan had struck a reporter in Algiers as sufficiently sensational to write an article about it in his paper. He took it all with a grain of salt. If only he had known how much more salt there was in it!

The beginning of my journey was inauspicious. As I

looked out of the train window in the morning we were in the northern desert of Algeria. For local color there was nothing but a row of telephone poles and, at long intervals, stark walled-in military barracks. A nosy colonial officer, obviously a Germanic Alsatian, started a conversation with me and ended up by asking me a lot of questions in an effort to nail me as a spy.

"How does it happen that you speak French without an accent?" he asked me with a nasty kind of camaraderie. "Do you speak other languages? Russian, perhaps?"

I wonder what sinister motives he would have attributed to my intention of traveling with a caravan, if I had told him about it.

There was no vacancy in the good hotel in Colomb-Béchar, and in the other one, quite a few steps lower in scale, the man behind the counter—thin, pale and fish-eyed—took pleasure in telling me that he had no room either, while a hydrocephaloid dwarf kept twitching and bothering me on my right and a seedy tubercular shoved a large dried lizard under my nose from the left. "Souvenir? Souvenir?"

On the assumption that no man-made problem is insoluble I looked elsewhere and eventually found a room.

There were no caravans in this northern part of the desert. They told me I would have to wait two weeks for the trans-Saharan truck, scheduled to leave once a month, to take me farther south. One day, after wandering about in the oasis, I found a message in my room requesting me to call on the military commander. Remembering the blockhead in the train, I feared the worst. I braced myself with a clean shirt

The Road to Gao · 63

and marched down to headquarters, ready to defend my innocence to the last. After ten tantalizing minutes of uncertainty the commander received me in his private quarters and immediately offered me a drink. He had read the article about me in the Algiers newspaper and had looked forward to meeting the *orientaliste américain*. We got on famously.

"So you are really going into the desert?" he said. *"Eh bien,* I hope you know what you are doing. I love the Sahara myself. I can understand your enthusiasm. But it is nothing to play with, you know. People still get lost. Of course, you have a desert in America, too; in California, I think? Ah, you Americans, you have everything!"

I reminded him that we didn't have camel caravans, and that that was why I had come to the Sahara.

"Evidently," he said, "the first requisite for joining a caravan is to find one."

He was keenly interested in art, and I was so relieved by his cordial reception that I decided to show my appreciation by presenting him with a drawing which I had done of the market place. On the day of my departure from Colomb-Béchar I called again at headquarters and explained my errand to the two native sentinels. *Monsieur le Commandant,* I learned, was out of town. In that case, I asked—inadvertently taking a step forward—could I leave this package in his office? The sentinel in front of me dropped the corners of his mustache, frowned viciously and barred the way. At the same instant something tickled me in the back. I turned my head. It was the point of the other guard's bayonet.

"Well," I said, "never mind. Will you please see to it that this drawing is delivered to him?"

The truck was to leave at noon. A clerk checked my papers and made sure that I had a yellow fever vaccination. Larbi, the driver, a rather unorthodox Arab of enormous proportions dressed in a voluminous pair of very dirty native trousers, radiated good will.

"Always glad to have someone with me," he said in fluent French, "provided they are prepared for the worst. Sometimes, you know, we get stuck, and it may be a few days before we get going again. You are not in a hurry, are you? I once had a lady on this trip. I told her: 'Lady, I want you to know this is no taxicab.' She said: 'Listen, you big ape, I have been in tougher spots.' I said: 'Yeah, but it probably wasn't outdoors.' And sure enough, she complained right away, after two days, how rough it was, and dusty, and that the truck smelled bad. And then she got sick on top of it. I don't know what I would have done with her if she hadn't caught a ride back from Adrar. I always say: Ladies belong in bed. I don't want to have anything to do with them on the job. Where are you going?"

"To Gao, unless I can find a caravan sooner."

"A caravan? Billah? God's truth? Well, if you think you can go on a caravan I guess you can travel in this crate."

All trans-Saharan trucks have names. Larbi's was called *Luciole,* glow-worm, something of a euphemism for a ten-ton truck.

Larbi took off as if he intended to reach the Congo by nightfall. We got as far as Kersaz: a resthouse and a few

The Road to Gao • *65*

hovels in the sand. A long hot drive the second day brought us to what looked like a setting for a colonial exposition: the tremendous square of Adrar, flanked by massive buildings and colonnades in deep red clay. A surprisingly clean rest-house in the miserable hamlet of Reggan was our next stop. From here on south stretched the fearsome Tanezrouft, an absolutely flat and barren desert of coarse gravel.

In 1923 the first expedition sponsored by the French automobile manufacturer Citroën crossed the region. The five armored caterpillar cars traveled in close formation for fear of a sudden attack by Reguibat, wild tribesmen from Spanish Río de Oro, who still terrorized this part of the desert when there was any sign of a prize.

Théodore Monod, the famous French scientist and explorer, traversed the widest part of the Tanezrouft from west to east in 1936. He found it "sterile to a degree that can hardly be found elsewhere," so flat that "a stone, if there had been one, would have assumed the proportions of a mountain." A legend has it that, somewhere, buried in this inferno, are the ruins of two ancient cities, Tokalet and Tafassaset.

"Talk about your caravan!" said Larbi. "Nobody will ever know how many poor devils have been cooked alive in this charming place. White people, too. A professor came down here in 1942. He and his guide got lost. They found a waterhole, but it was all fouled up with magnesium. The professor couldn't stand it any longer and drank the water anyway. His guide had more sense. He didn't drink the water because he saw that the camels wouldn't touch it. Naturally, the professor died. The guide tied himself to his camel and let it go where he knew it would go. It turned up at a good well in a military post, and the guy was saved. Even so, I'll stick to the road. Nothing can happen as long as we stick to the road."

Larbi dozed at the wheel. There was no sign of life and it didn't matter if the truck went off the trail half a mile. We had been rattling along for three hours when we became aware of a black spot ahead. As we approached, it turned out to be a lone Negro who waved frantically, then fell to the ground and, with pitiful gestures of supplication, crawled on his hands and knees toward us. He was quite delirious. Larbi stopped the truck and dabbed the man's face and lips with a wet rag. Later he stowed him away among the boxes of merchandise. We stopped several times to give him small quantities of water to drink.

"In a case like this," Larbi told me, "you have to be careful. Just a little at a time. Not too much. If you give them too much, they kick the bucket just when you think they are going to snap out of it."

From the hysterical account the poor fellow gave in a lingo that even Larbi could hardly understand, it transpired that he had been lost for two days without water when he found the road. No one had come along, so he had stumbled on in the direction of Reggan, ninety miles to the north. If we had not rescued him, he would have died that night. Two hours' drive farther south Larbi let him off at a point from which he only had to walk twenty miles to the nearest camp.

"At least," said Larbi, "there *was* a camp—last year."

It took us thirteen hours from Reggan to Bidon V, Can

Number Five, so named after an oil drum left as a marker by an early expedition. It now consists of half a dozen small Quonset huts, an airplane beacon (out of commission) and a dry well.

Bright and early, we continued past wrecked trucks and occasional graves among the tire tracks. Then, a week after our departure from Colomb-Béchar, a few thorn trees appeared, gazelles bounded about in the early morning, beautiful black women stood like statues among round huts and termite heaps, goats and humped cattle stampeded at the sight of the roaring monster away into the golden savanna of the Sudan.

2 Najim

THE CAMEL'S WORST ENEMY, THE GASOLINE ENGINE, IS CREEPING farther and farther into the desert, but there are still a few areas left where automobiles cannot pass. In these regions there are no travel agencies, and the natives hate to commit themselves to any definite time or place. If you inquire, they will say: Yes, a caravan will be leaving soon—and cautiously qualify the affirmation with *inshallah*. Now Allah's will is notoriously unpredictable; more likely than not you are left with the strong suspicion that divine providence may call the whole thing off. In the circumstances I was very fortunate to meet an understanding French administrator, Monsieur Chénal, in Gao on the Niger, who introduced me to an Arab gentleman with a firm mind: Sidna Ali, a wealthy trader.

Sidna Ali received us on the roof of his house in Gao and served us tea. After the slap-happy Larbi he gave the impression of a man of consequence with his neat turban, his snow-white robe, his good manners. Below us, beyond the mango trees, native craft were gliding down the channels of the Niger and shiny Songhaï women carrying calabashes on their heads filed to the river where they stripped to the waist to do their washing. The rose-colored dunes, miles away on the opposite shore, appeared deceivingly close.

Reclining on leather cushions, we assured each other of the excellent state of our health and, in keeping with good Arab manners, loudly slurped the sweet mint tea. When the required period of greetings had expired, my friend, Monsieur Chénal, casually brought the conversation around to caravans.

"Well, how are your affairs getting along?" he asked.

"Things are a little slow at the moment," said Sidna Ali, "because so many of the roads have been washed out by the last tornado, and the trucks are delayed."

"That wouldn't stop camels from getting through, would it?"

"Oh, no, a caravan can go through where a truck gets stuck, but it takes a little longer."

"Have you ever been with a caravan?" I asked.

"Yes," said Sidna Ali, "I have been on many caravans, and so has my father before me. My grandfather, Aghada, came as a slave with the caravan of Pasha Djouder from Morocco to the Sudan. That was a very long trip! One day the caravan stopped at a well. My grandfather and four other slaves were performing their prayers when the Pasha passed by. He noticed that Aghada prayed with such fervor that the fetters fell from his wrists. Now, Aghada had never revealed his name to his master. The Pasha demanded to know who he was. My grandfather said: 'I am Aghada.'

"The Pasha remembered that he had been told in Morocco before his departure into the desert that he would find a man at this well named Aghada who would advise him in what direction to proceed. Aghada told him to travel to Gao and Timbuctoo.

"The Pasha apologized for the hardships he had imposed on his slave and set Aghada free. My grandfather continued toward the Niger where he intended to establish a town. He came to the river between Goundam and Timbuctoo. As he bowed to the earth in prayer, he found that his forehead would always be pricked by *cram-cram,* a plant full of terrible burs. So he decided to travel north again, the way he had come, until he reached the clean desert sand, and there, with his followers, he founded the town of Araouan."

Inwardly inclined, in this particular case, to agree with Henry Ford that "history is bunk," I said: "Sidna, that is a fine story. But tell me, how is it possible that your grandfather lived at the time of Pasha Djouder? I thought that he came to the Sudan three hundred and sixty years ago?"

"*Aiwa,*" said Sidna, "that is true, but, you see, Aghada was my *first* grandfather."

"What do you know about this year's salt caravan?" asked my French friend, coming down to earth.

"The *azalaï* will start very soon. My camels are now in

Araouan. All the camels have gone north and mine will return loaded with salt from Taoudéni along with the others."

"Sidna Ali," I said, "I would like to travel with the *azalaï*. Do you think this could be done?"

"It can be done," he answered, "if *you* can do it."

Monsieur Chénal reminded me that there remained the problem of getting to the north, to Taoudéni. At the same time he remembered that a military patrol in desert trucks was due to go on reconnaissance in that direction. He would find out if they could take me. "And by the way," he added, "you will need a *goumier* [native guard] to go along with you. I will pick one out who can speak French."

All this was very encouraging. Next, there was the question of procuring two camels to return with the caravan.

"You will need four camels," said Sidna Ali. "One for you, one for the *goumier*, one to carry your provisions, and one to carry the water skins."

Here we were getting down to money. This was the test. With anyone else I would have had serious misgivings, but Sidna Ali had such an ingratiating, open face that I instinctively knew he could be trusted, even if his imagination was sometimes a little ahead of the facts.

"Could I make an arrangement with you for the loan of four good camels?"

"*Aiwa*, I will give you a letter to a man in Taoudéni who will furnish the camels. You can pay me half the cost now and the rest when you return. One hundred francs* for each camel per day. All my camels are good ones."

Monsieur Chénal's glance convinced me that this was

* French colonial francs. $1.00 : 170 francs C.F.A. (Colonies Françaises d'Afrique).

indeed a fair price. Trying to think of everything, I wondered what would happen if one of the camels broke down.

"In that case," said Sidna Ali, "I will replace it immediately."

The officer in charge of the military patrol regretfully informed me that it was against regulations to transport a civilian. My hopes of going with the caravan had all but faded when Najim, the *goumier,* appeared. He was a dark leathery little man of bone and muscle with a lean face framed in a deep blue turban and a well-oiled beard, his loose *dera* gathered by a Sam Browne belt over the thinnest waist in Africa; a typical man of the desert: quick as a ferret, tough as catgut, with the eyes of a killer and a little boy's smile. He was very polite. After talking to me for a while and studying me with his brilliant black eyes he became quite optimistic about his assignment. In response to my worries over the business of getting to Taoudéni he took the Napoleonic view: *tout est possible,* and over our first smoke together he had me convinced that an American and a Beidani made an unbeatable combination.

"First," he said, "we need many things. We must have provisions for two months. We must have good *guerbas* [water skins]. Do you have a saddle? No. We must find one. Do you have rope? We must have plenty of rope for the pack camels. But don't worry. I will do everything for you and I will tell you all you want to know."

The following two days we were in and out of the native stores until we had collected great quantities of rope, two flashlights, two blankets, extra sandals, a second-hand saddle, a pair of hideous socks Najim wanted in the worst way, plus

        100 lbs. rice
         12 lbs. green tea
         20 lbs. sugar (in cones of 4 lbs. each)
         20 lbs. noodles
         40 packages dehydrated soups
         12 cans sardines
          4 quarts butter (rancid)
          5 lbs. crude tobacco
          2 bags charcoal
             Cigarettes (French)

Canned goods—never used by the nomads themselves—had to be avoided on account of their weight. For meat we would have to rely on the wild game of the region: gazelles and antelopes. I had my doubts that we would see an addax, a species of antelope as big as a cow which roams alone through inaccessible parts of the desert. Najim had the necessary cooking utensils. He let the word go out that we were in the market for *guerbas*. We were besieged at once by sorry old men, sly camel drivers, and large numbers of black ragamuffins who exhibited all varieties of goatskins, many with holes in them, some shedding hair, some so dried up and brittle that they fell apart in our hands, some that had been stripped from animals that were sick to begin with. Our standing offer was two hundred and fifty francs apiece, take it or leave it. Out of the lot we chose four that promised to hold water.

There was only one thing more that Najim insisted upon:

a wooden box with a lock. There was no necessity for it; Najim knew better than I did that a wooden box was an awkward object for a camel to carry. The point was that, in a country where everything is toted about in leather bags, a wooden box would lend us prestige, and Najim was greatly concerned with impressing his fellow men with the fact that he was traveling in the company of an important personage. The box, the size of a baby coffin, had to be made especially according to his specifications; the cost was out of all proportion to the quality of the workmanship and to its need.

By an extraordinary stroke of luck I became acquainted with two French scientists from Dakar who were on a geological expedition headed for the Taoudéni region. They were not interested in rock salt, but were planning to make a surface study for oil a little to the north of Taoudéni. I learned from them that this area was low plateau country in the *djouf*, "the stomach," the most god-forsaken section of the Sahara, and truly one of the most remote: about 1,300 miles northeast of Dakar as the crow flies, 460 miles west of Bidon V, 1,100 miles south of Marrakech (Morocco), 550 miles north of Timbuctoo. It was a depression, about 700 feet above sea level which, according to Théodore Monod (who had been everywhere) was "the result of a local geological accident due to the existence of natural dikes which had closed it off and retained portions of the hydraulic flow." The formation was Quaternary, the bottom of a dead inland sea. The precipitation was less than ten millimeters per annum. It was one of the hottest places in the world during nine months of the year, with temperatures up to 127 degrees in the shade.

Ever since the Songhaï Negro kings of the upper Niger condemned their slaves to work in the infamous mines, the Taoudéni salt pan has had the reputation of hell on earth. From the beginning of the eleventh century, salt had been extracted at Teghaza, to the north, but, due to relentless warfare between the Songhaï from the Sudan and the Berbers from Morocco, it fell into decay. In 1352 an Arab traveler found Teghaza "an unattractive village," and Taoudéni, which has been exploited since the sixteenth century, was no improvement. It has one well of evil water, highly purgative, which even Pasha Djouder's seasoned mercenaries couldn't take. In a contemporary chronicle, the Tarikh es-Sudan, Abderrahman Sadi, the celebrated seventeenth-century scholar of Timbuctoo, records the history of the Sudan up to the year 1652. In speaking of Pasha Djouder's passage at Taoudéni, the author informs us that "the water, attacking the men's intestines, caused dysentery and killed many of them apart from those who perished in combat."

Three French officers at the head of a military detachment were the first Europeans to visit Taoudéni in 1906. There was consternation among the desert tribes when the French established military posts five years later at Taoudéni, El Guettar and Telig. In retaliation against this unexpected interference, the natives abandoned the peaceful trade in salt and took to gun-running via the Canary Islands and Río de Oro. The French army posts, under constant attack, forgotten by the colonial administration and without supplies, had to be evacuated by the few who remained alive. The Blue Moors of Río de Oro, who are believed to be related to the Tuareg, were in the forefront of the fight. They were so successful in their raids upon the French and upon Moslems who had submitted to the French, that most of the camel men, who had so far stuck to the caravan trade, joined the outlaws. This situation continued for nearly forty years. It was not until 1935, after the French conquest of Tindouf, in the north, that the route from Morocco into Mauritania could be used again with any safety. Out of one hundred and thirty warriors during one of the last great Moorish raids into the Sudan, ten were taken prisoner, thirty were killed, and seventy died of thirst on their flight through the desert. The "pagans" meant business. The odds were too great. It was better to settle down to the caravan trade.

3   The Town Built of Salt

AFTER AFFIXING MY SIGNATURE TO A STATEMENT DECLARING THAT they could not be held responsible for any harm that might come to me, the geologists agreed to take not only me along but Najim, saddles, provisions and all. Monsieur Chénal gave me a general letter of introduction in Arabic to native chiefs I might encounter, which read:

To all readers of the present letter
Greetings and Benedictions and the Mercy of Allah.
The writer of these words asks that his friend, an honorable
gentleman, be given every assistance during his voyage.
Allah will reward your kindness.

الى من يقرأ هذا الكتاب السلام
التام ومباركة و رحمة الله وبعد
يطلب كاتب الحروف ان
تعوذوا ما هبى السيد المحترم
النكول بي سيرة و جزكم الله
بخير على ما تفعلوا بي ذلك

و السلام

كُتب بكلو ١٠/١١/١٩٥٤

جرال حاكم

The written word has great persuasive power with the nomads, very few of them being able to read and write themselves.

In a driving rain we started for the desert: two Frenchmen, their native guide, myself, Najim, and two black boys in a Landrover and two Dodge Power Wagons equipped with sand tires and long steel ladders for traction in case the cars bogged down.

During this trip of eight days' duration we set our course by charts and compass, and by the rare landmarks pointed out by the guide. It was only at exceptional intervals that the terrain allowed smoother going than a painful grinding in low gear which frayed the nerves and stupefied the mind. Occasionally the Landrover ahead veered in pursuit of a gazelle. When an animal had been dropped, Najim would dash over to it to cut its throat and watch the blood flow from the gaping wound with joyful sensuality. As a Moslem, he could eat game only if slain by a Moslem, and if Allah's name had been mentioned over the dying animal. The geologists were very generous with their supplies and masters at preparing a *filet flambé au cognac*.

Late one afternoon we saw a caravan in the distance, a silhouette in miniature of swaying camels and men in flowing robes, leisurely skirting a dune, the wide world before them. What a much more dignified mode of travel theirs was compared to ours! How noble and confident these men looked, even so far away!

When we stopped for our last snack en route, the guide made a triumphant double-armed gesture in the proper direction and announced: "Taoudéni, *hock*!"

Azalaï · *78*

Shortly after we came to the rim of the vast depression which had furnished salt for the Sudan for so many centuries: a dismal plain fading into a pale pink haze with a low *gara* (table mountain) here and there, flanked in the northeast by the slopes of the Hamada El Haricha.

We camped for the night in the lee of a dune halfway between the mines of Agorgott and the walled hamlet of Smeida, situated in the middle of the *sebkhra* (salt pan) which is known as Taoudéni.

In the early morning we had a look at Smeida, a small fortified village, about three hundred years old, with crumbling walls and the remnants of five watchtowers. Within the walls was mostly rubble. The old men of Smeida had become "sons of the shadow," as the nomads call those who can no longer follow the caravan trail of sun and wind.

Then we drove the four and a half miles across the Taoudéni plain to the mining village of Agorgott. We were quickly surrounded by an excited mob of Sudanese and a great swarm of flies, and presently by a number of Arabs including one who introduced himself as the local "guardian of the peace." While Najim and I unloaded our equipment and provisions, the geologists made the tour of Agorgott and then bid us good-by. We were now on our own.

Prompted by his good sense of diplomacy, Najim explained the reason for our presence to Madaoua, the guardian of the peace, and handed him my Arabic letter of introduction. The policeman became very official, puffed himself up and made a great show of scanning the document. The only thing that was wrong with his stern attitude was the fact that he held the letter upside down. While outwardly trying to maintain a calm severity, as befitted the occasion, he was torn by a profound inner struggle. He might have saved his face had he pretended to be satisfied with the contents of the letter, but his curiosity got the better of him and so, before the assembled crowd, he had to deflate himself to the extent of asking Najim to read it aloud.

The man to whom Sidna Ali had given us a letter was one of the bystanders, one Moulay Zeidane, an Arab of far greater intelligence than the blustering policeman. He said that he would consider it a privilege to loan us a house for as long as we should wish to stay. This gave the guardian of the peace the opportunity to repair his damaged pride by asserting his authority. In a flash he had commanded all able-bodied Sudanese to pick up our baggage. They fell upon it, lifted it on their heads, and carried it safari-style along a narrow path between deep holes to what turned out to be a Count-of-Monte-Christo dungeon. I gave them each a cigarette which made them literally dance with joy.

The town of Agorgott is unique in that it is constructed entirely of blocks of salt, the low-grade refuse from the mines. The dilapidated cubicles that are the houses stand among a wild confusion of pits and mounds, hardly distinguishable from the surrounding rubble, as if they had risen out of the churned-up ground from the debris of a battlefield after a heavy shelling. Over all drifts a stench of rotten eggs due to hydrogen disulphide in the water which seeps up from the bottom of the salt mines: thousands of excavations set close together, some active and many of them abandoned, from the center of town far out into the desert, each thirty feet square and twenty-five feet deep.

Like all the other houses and dugouts that sheltered perhaps twenty Arab traders and a hundred Sudanese, ours stood beside one of these pits filled with bones, rotten skins, fragments of mats, goat skulls, broken gourds and excrement. The jagged, hammered-out side of an oil drum served as a door. Ducking through the low opening from the glare outside, the interior presented a pitch-black cave with sand underfoot and the odor of a hole used for all purposes. A few shafts of light stabbed through cracks between the rough blocks of salt, revealing a frayed rag on the smoke-blackened ceiling and a string of mealy worms on a mission underground. The buzzing of untold flies sounded like a distant waterfall.

While Najim busily arranged our things and spread out our palmetto sleeping mats I stepped out for a breath of air. On examining the exterior of the house more closely I noticed that the carcass of a camel had been incorporated as roofing material. The legs had been arranged advantageously and the skin beaten down between the hips and chest. The mummified head reposed on the edge of the wall, the long eyebrows waving in the breeze. It made the famous Parisian nightclub Le Boeuf sur le Toit—the Ox on the Roof—seem rather commonplace.

The flies were unendurable, but I was at a loss what to do as there was no such thing as a nail to hang up a mosquito net in the house. Najim, the great improviser, picked up a rope and anchored it outside, brought it in through the door, across the cave, and out again through a hole in the wall, providing a perfect support for the net. With a little practice it was possible to slip under it without letting more than a dozen flies enter at the same time. I lay down to meditate upon the melancholy scene.

Najim had no sooner left me alone, than some of the black miners timidly came to the door, pointing to their suppurating sores. These were perfectly round, the size of a quarter and half an inch deep, as if they had been stamped out with a cooky die. All I could think of was to shake some sulpha powder into the holes and put large Band-aids over the ghastly wounds. The Negroes were delighted with the Band-aids on their legs, offered a soft "*amrack*" (thank you) and went back to the salt pits with exaggerated hopes.

Many of the early explorers were medical men who won the confidence of the natives with their skill and their good deeds. In remote parts of Africa the belief still persists that all white men are doctors.

Najim returned from a tour of inspection with a Roman lamp, a small earthenware dish with a wick floating in shea butter. He suggested that we let it burn all night to keep away vipers and scorpions.

"This reminds me," I said, "there don't seem to be many camels."

"Oh, yes, there are many camels, on the other side."

For a moment I was wondering if he was speaking metaphysically, meaning in another world, but he added, "The caravans camp to the east, and many camels are on pasture, far from here. Don't worry, all you want to see, I show you."

Outside, hooded figures were wandering among the

mounds. One of them came toward our enclosure, a Sudani at his heels who was dragging something by his side. It was our host who came to offer us a broad smile and a live sheep. Now we could invite all the notables to dinner.

The Sudani returned in the morning to butcher the sheep, and Najim informed me, "One shoulder and the skin we give to Moulay Zeidane; the stomach and the head, we give to the butcher."

By this time there wasn't an Arab merchant, Berber tribesman or Negro miner who had not made the pilgrimage to our house. An American in Taoudéni had about the same effect that Flying Saucermen usually have in California.

Arab traders from Timbuctoo and Araouan spend several months out of the year in Taoudéni to supervise the working of their mines and the distribution of the salt. As a sideline some of them keep a stock of merchandise in their dingy holes: rice, millet, sugar, tea, pots and *guerbas*—all worth their weight in gold at this distance from any commercial center. Articles of trade and all provisions are brought to Taoudéni twice a year by caravans.

Anyone who can furnish the labor may open a mine. The black workers fall into two categories:

"Captives" (still so called by the Arabs), now kept servants, who are entitled to extract for themselves what salt they can two days out of seven; they receive no pay but, if they have left families behind, they are taken care of by their masters.

"Freemen," who are stuck in the mine to pay off debts, also entitled to two days' work out of seven for themselves; they get a small wage but are responsible for their kin.

The specialists who split the extracted blocks of salt and shape them into bars receive no pay and have to take care of themselves, but out of every four bars they get one. The unskilled worker who hauls clay away or dumps out water gets next to nothing and has no privileges. The working methods have not changed since the Middle Ages. Squatting, or standing with bare, lacerated feet in the corrosive brine at the bottom of the pits, the miners hack away the stinking clay with broad hoes. Clubs with a spike on the end serve to cut the blocks of salt in the rough; a narrow hoe is used to trim the slabs down to a thickness of one inch and a half, a width of fourteen inches, a length of four feet. The finished bar weighs between fifty and sixty-five pounds. It takes four men one month to dig down to the strata of salt. Here, where it is least desirable, water collects. This is carried out of the pits in goatskins. Frequently miners follow a vein along flooded side tunnels barely high enough for a man to crawl on all fours. The layers of salt are of varying quality; the finest slabs are hard as marble and crystal-clear. The tools used to extract and trim the slabs of salt are made and kept in repair by the *forgeron*, the native blacksmith.

Absolutely nothing can be grown in Taoudéni, and there is no use in boiling the foul water from the well because it merely concentrates the salt and magnesium content. One of the Sudanese workmen became a celebrity as the only inhabitant known to have ever suffered from constipation, yet a shipwrecked American sailor named Adams who was taken prisoner by the Arabs, sold into slavery in 1810, and later escaped, claimed to have passed through the region with a caravan and gave this account:

Azalaï • *84*

The market place of Ghardaïa

1b. The oasis of In Salah

2a.   Tuareg of the Hoggar

2b.   Méha

3a. Dagh Rahli nobles of the Hoggar

3b. Amenokal Baï (right), the Supreme Chief of the Tuareg

4a. A salt pit at Taoudéni

4b. Business section: Ago

Camels assembled for the caravan at Taoudéni

5b. Our camels being loaded for the departure

6a.   The caravan on the march

6b.   Our camp at Krenac

. Camel tracks

7b.   A casualty

8a. A waterhole in the southern Sahara;
goatskins in the foreground

8b. Camels being lined up for a carava

Bani

9b. Najim filling a goatskin at a waterhole

10a. The caravan in the red sand

10b. Graves of Berabish camelmen killed by the Regι

A pasture at sunset

13b. The last halt

14a. Abaradyou: the caravan terminal at Timbuctoo

14b. Main Street: Timbuct

15a. Tuareg warrior striding through the market place in Timbuctoo

15b. Customers for the salt from Taoudéni

16a. Marouchet

16b. Aguibou

16d. Master of a pe[a]
caravan, Nigeria

16c. The author (hands badly swollen
from heat and insect bites)

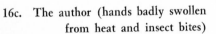

A supply of excellent water, and the fertility it produces, render this a valuable place of refreshment for travelers across the desert. It contains also numerous beds of salt, an article in universal demand over Sudan. Taudeny is a large village inhabited by Moors and negroes, who are both equally black; its neighborhood is cultivated like that of Timbuctoo, and abounds with date and fig trees.

Mr. Adams, I am afraid, was a liar who had never seen the place.

The only green as far as the eye could see was a patch of poisonous weeds of which Najim said: "It is called lub'feina. If you touch it, you go crazy; if you eat it, you die."

He pointed out to me a babbling lunatic. "You see that man? He touched some, by mistake."

4   Camels and Reguibat

AS NAJIM HAD PREDICTED, THERE WERE MANY CAMELS ALONG the eastern fringe of the salt pits, and certainly more nomads than there were townspeople: lean Berabish from the southern desert, handsome Moors from the north, Kounta from Adrar des Iforas and tall and solemn Tuareg, each group loosely centered around its own baggage. Some of the men had just arrived and relaxed over a pot of tea, others, preparing to depart, were busy tying wet strips of rawhide around slabs of salt, linking two together at the long ends so that they would balance each other slung over an animal's back. Small groups sat eating out of a common bowl, chucking bones over their shoulders after the manner of Henry the Eighth. Water skins, the most important item of equipment of a caravan, lay about among stacked pack saddles, sacks of rice and millet, and grimy butter gourds. There were no tents; the men slept in the open on torn raffia mats, their heads on their *tassoufra,* fringed and decorated leather bags that contained all their personal necessities. Scattered over this ancient campsite were skeletal remains and blobs of desiccated entrails. Some of the camels, exhausted after a long journey, were lying on their sides, neck and legs stretched full length in the sand. There were dark and woolly camels from Morocco, small and badly galled ones from the south, and a few fine riding camels of the Tuareg, the most conceited of the lot. Most of them stood, hobbled and perplexed, in a resigned stupor; some, kneeling, chewed the cud with a go-to-hell air; some milled about with a view to stealing a mouthful of fodder from the forage piles despite repeated cracks from a driver's club. Couched animals groaned furiously when they were made to get up, standing ones growled bitterly when they were pulled down. All of them greeted the mere approach of man with a snarl, and many had differences among themselves for there were frequent screams and sudden leaps as one disgruntled animal savagely nipped its nearest neighbor. Some lay with their muzzles tied up to prevent them from ruminating. This preserved the moisture in their bodies. The camel men have a theory that it weakens the animals if they are watered too frequently. Given the scarcity of wells, there isn't much temptation to overdo it.

Azalaï • *86*

Back at the dungeon I told Najim that a caravan was about to leave and that we had better get ready. Of course, he knew all about it; it wasn't *our* caravan. They were people from Kidal, he said disparagingly. To a Berabish anything that smells of Tuareg is anathema. So he kept on cooking his rice in a black fog of flies.

Apparently, the guardian of the peace had got a whiff of it; he came all but running. Moulay Zeidane arrived in a huge two-toned turban and brought a friend, a gentle *marabout* —a holy man, versed in the Koran, and one who usually possesses *baraka*, a beneficial supernatural power. The Caid, the most venerable personage, came last and settled himself on the mat very slowly and with great dignity.

That old boy was worth a second look, a discreet one, because he was so scarred up and had no nose. Here was a warrior of the old school, whatever side he had been on. Could he be persuaded to tell about some of his battles? Preferably about the one which had cost him his nose? The hitch was how to make these fellows talk when they never touched anything stronger than tea. He was eighty, conservatively, with a twinkle in his bright eyes to make the angels blush. He looked at me pretty closely, too, the first American to visit Taoudéni, rumored to have lived with the Tuareg, interested in camels, a fellow warrior. He wasn't given to small talk. He didn't ask me: How do you like Taoudéni? He knew that no one could possibly like it.

Najim had placed the bowl of rice before us and lit a candle. The policeman was already working on a hunk of mutton with one hand; with the other one he clutched his most prized possession, something he only exposed to public view during rare functions: a cheap alarm clock, which he could not read. A gallery of captives sat in a semicircle in the darkness just outside the door.

"You come from America?" Moulay Zeidane asked. "That is where big trucks come from. I have read about Detroit."

I agreed that trucks were made in Detroit, but couldn't guess what this had to do with me.

"Perhaps you come from Detroit?" He pronounced it "Detro-ah," the French way.

I told him that I did not.

"I thought perhaps you came to see if you could transport our salt in trucks?"

So that was it! They were afraid that I had come to mechanize and ruin their economy!

I assured Moulay Zeidane that I had not the slightest intention of interfering with their business and that, on the contrary, my sole interest lay in observing a way of life that had not changed for many centuries. My attitude was unexpectedly confirmed by the guardian of the peace, who said: "*Ouallah!* I saw him among the camels today!"

"Yes, in fact, I would like to know where *our* camels are. Sidna Ali told me that I could rely on you, Moulay Zeidane. Will you be sure to have four camels for us?"

"The best, with strong legs and firm hump! I will choose them myself. You will have them tomorrow!"

"And there will be a caravan that we can join?"

"There are caravans all the time, until the great heat. Then, only the captives remain in Taoudéni."

The *marabout* popped riceballs in his mouth with wonderful dexterity. He had fine features and a very dark skin, probably owing to a strong mixture of Songhaï. He asked me: "Are there people as black as I am in your country?"

The Caid gave me a look as much as to say: What difference does that make? Are we going to judge one another by appearances?

I told the *marabout*: "Not only black, but red ones, too."

The Caid thought that was a good joke. Moulay Zeidane wanted to know if there were any camels in Detroit. And did we have a desert, as in Africa? I did the best I could to give them a general idea of the things that are familiar to us. They were impressed when I told them about tall buildings, refrigerators, traffic lights, teabags, inner-spring mattresses, paved roads over which trucks could travel a thousand miles in three days. In the end they said incredulously, "And yet, there are no camels!"

I offered everyone a cigarette. The Caid didn't light his, but stuck it upright in the sand.

"I understand that there has been a good deal of fighting around Taoudéni in the past."

"Yes," he said, speaking in Arabic, "before the French took over we had lots of trouble with the Reguibat. They were always attacking our caravans."

"Were you ever attacked?"

"Yes, but, *Hamdullah*, I was spared the worst. This happened long ago. We were only three days north from here and all went well up from Araouan, but we had an uneasy feeling because, when we started on this journey, our guide had seen a lone raven in the sky. We didn't want to wait any longer; it was in the month of June and the camels walk slowly in the heat. As a precaution we had a man ride along

Camels and Reguibat · 89

each side of the caravan to warn us of any marauders who might be in the vicinity. So far they had seen no sign of anyone. There was nothing to worry about during the day; it was in the darkness that we felt we were being watched. In the desert, a shadow at night is often more dangerous than a stranger met in the daytime; each night we felt there were shadows watching us. It was on the seventh night that one of our guards thought he saw something move far out to the west, but nothing happened, and when he rode out in the morning to the place where he believed someone had been, he could find no tracks.

" '*Zrohr*!' he said. 'Ghosts!'

"We continued all that day with the sand in our faces and the wind blinding us until evening, when the air cleared again. Then we all saw a rider far away to the west, following our camel train at the same speed. We stopped, couched the camels, and sat waiting with our guns. In the dark our scouts rode to the sides and to the rear. There was no sign of a rider, and they found no tracks.

"*Zrohr*! No doubt about it.

"We continued for four days and almost forgot our fears. But on the fifth day, at dawn, we found ourselves surrounded by a band of Reguibat. They were no *zrohr*; they were real. One of their scouts had followed us at a distance of two days' ride from his party. He had informed them about our caravan. Now more and more of them appeared out of the wind. They greeted us in the name of Allah and politely inquired about our health. We assured them of our well-being and expressed the hope that they were in want of nothing beyond any man's due. They said, no, they never looked for more than what came their way, thanks to Allah.

"Their leader had a bad bullet hole in his leg. When one of our men told him that I was good at curing wounds, we stopped and the Reguibat sheik was helped down from his mount. I gave instructions to my men to light a fire and cut open the man's leg to let it bleed for a while. Then I washed out the wound with boiled camel urine, and when it was nice and clean, I held my gunbarrel over the fire until it got red-hot and pushed it down into the bullet hole. 'It may happen that ye hate a thing which is good for you, and it may happen that ye love a thing which is bad for you; Allah knoweth, ye know not.'

"All that day the Reguibat rode along with us until we arrived at a well. There they slashed our sacks of merchandise, a few shots were fired, two of our camels were killed, six of our men bled to death in the sand. Our guide had run away and kept shooting from behind a rock. He killed one of the Reguibat before they dropped him. He was wounded in the head and he begged them to finish him off, but they paid no attention to him and sat down to drink tea. When they were through with it they rounded up and loaded all the animals. Then—Allah preserve us from man's cruelty!—they skinned one of the dead camels, tied our guide inside the skin, and left him to dry up in it.

" 'As for you,' said the leader of the Reguibat to me, 'you can keep this camel and this sack of dates—and tell your Christian friends to come and see us in Río de Oro!'

"At the time I didn't know the country in the north too well. I decided to follow our tracks back. By the second day the wind had left nothing to guide me, but if I had not found my way in the end I would not be here to tell you about it."

The Caid pulled the cigarette out of the sand, held it to the candle, and leaned back behind a cloud of smoke. From that adventure he had escaped unscathed. It was evident that he had been a very handsome man in his day; too bad he did not get around to an account of the event which had earned him those alarming battle scars. Najim—playing "master of the Sahara"—had taken his gun out of the dust cover and was still blowing at the breech and rubbing the stock with a corner of his *djellabah* when the guardian of the peace departed with his alarm clock and the Caid, Moulay Zeidane and the *marabout* took their leave, followed by the captives.

"I suppose it was in another skirmish that the Caid lost his nose?" I asked Najim.

"No," he said. "He did not lose his nose in battle. The Caid knew a man who had a very beautiful wife. He fell in love with this woman, and while her husband was away, he always slept with the other man's wife. One day the husband found them together, so he took his knife and cut off the Caid's nose from the top down, and the woman's from the bottom up, and then he told the Caid that he could have her."

Next day the incredible happened: it rained. Under the low, gray sky the black men shivered in their rags, the narrow paths between the pits became ridges of slime, vile odors rose from the damp earth and the rats in the dungeon ran boldly in and out of crevices between the blocks of salt.

The Caid Oubba Ben Sidi Mohamed, Caid of Taoudéni, and the Brigadier Hammadi ould Mohamed, guardian of the Taoudéni mines, certify that Mr. Skolle is the first American to visit Taoudéni.

Signed at Taoudéni, French Sudan, December 10, 1954.

CAID OUBBA BEN SIDI MOHAMED
HAMMADI OULD MOHAMED
MOULAY ZEIDANE

Taoudéni had reached the peak of dreariness. Moulay Zeidane had said, "We are all surprised that you came to this place because it is very impossible." It was. I felt that if I scratched the ground lightly anywhere I would find something dead under it. There was no use in expecting our camels to show up; no caravan would depart in such weather.

Camels easily lose their footing on wet ground, being unused to it and not equipped to take hold on a slippery surface with their smooth pads.

The worst calamity the rain brought about was that it spoiled the camel droppings which are collected by the caravan men for fuel in the absence of wood. It was what Heinrich Barth, one of the first Saharan explorers, called "an unfavorable day," although Najim wasn't disturbed in the least. Since all activity had ceased in the mines and everyone had crawled into their holes, he found it a splendid opportunity to carry on a brisk trade in kola nuts. He had brought a large bag of them, carefully wrapped in damp cloth, and he spread delight wherever he chose to do business. Among manifold virtues, chewing kola nuts is believed to act as a stimulant, to serve as a medicament for dysentery, to ease the pains of hunger, and to function as an aphrodisiac. The last of these attributes was of little advantage in Taoudéni; there were only two women in the region, two old and emaciated Negroes.

Even in the brittle clarity of a normal day there was a frightful sadness about this woeful town which only showed a spark of life where the caravans camped against the broken, salt-encrusted outer crescent of the mines. The men were friendly and offered me tea as I wandered among them. In the course of a conversation I mentioned that I had heard so much about the Reguibat that I would like to see a member of that formidable tribe. The fellow I was speaking to smiled and said there were some Reguibat camped farther up the line, and that he would be glad to take me. We had not gone very far when a stalwart camel driver, draped in a dark blue *shandorah,* his face veiled Tuareg style, ambled up to chat with us.

"Here you are," said my companion. "He is a Reguibat."

I was properly impressed by the man and told him that I had heard a lot about his famous people. We had a good laugh together, drank some more tea, and when I told Najim later that I had met a Reguibat, and described the man who had introduced me, he too laughed and said: "The man you met first is a Reguibat himself."

5   *Departure of the Caravan*

THERE IS ONE QUALITY THAT AFRICA DEMANDS OF EVERY MAN: patience.

Nothing is ever simple, straightforward, or easy in Africa; nothing is ever quite as represented. In order to get along without nervous prostration one has to acquire a large reserve of tolerance and elasticity which, with practice, takes the place of a sixth sense in revaluating acts, conditions, statements, promises and people as so many shifting grains of sand.

Najim was greasing our goatskins and tying new rope to the four leg stumps on each one. I went out and inquired daily about the departure of the caravan, but never got a precise answer. The number of camels had greatly increased at the campground and salt bars were stacked ready to load along the entire east end of the mines. Large quantities of *houillas* lay on the ground—thick oblong pads made of coarse grass which fit around the hump of the camels under the wooden pack saddles. More and more animals were driven in from the distant pastures and from watering at the well at Smeida. Bloated as they were, they would have to rest for twenty-four hours. However, these preparations were significant and indeed there were rumors that the caravan would leave tomorrow. We still had not seen our camels, but we did have a new visitor, a weather-beaten nomad of Mongolian countenance with whom Najim had a previous acquaintance.

"This is Laazize," he said.

"Peace be with you, Laazize."

"He is coming with us."

"Fine."

"He is our *convoyeur*."

"Do we need a *convoyeur*?"

"Yes, because you and I are chiefs. We must have someone to take care of our camels. You only pay him as much as you do for a camel—one hundred francs a day—and Laazize is also a guide, so even if we are left behind by the caravan, we will not get lost."

This seemed quite reasonable, both in terms of cost and life insurance and, furthermore, as a good omen, for Laazize had inside information which indicated that the caravan would leave at six o'clock next morning.

At noon, the following day, he came running to announce, "The camels are there!" When I didn't see them, he corrected himself, "I mean they are coming." To say that they were "there" was a manner of speaking. Our camels were still ten miles away.

In the meantime we prepared and sorted our baggage for suitable loading and laid aside gifts of sugar and tea for our friends. They all appeared when Moulay Zeidane arrived with the camels: two enormous beasts, our mounts; a smaller one, but sturdy enough; and one—I thought—too young and inexperienced, and definitely antagonistic, especially toward the wooden box. The saddle animals merely winced a bit when they were couched, the veteran pack animal let out a few habitual groans, but when the wooden box was lashed to the portside of the little one, who didn't want to kneel in the first place, he snapped the hobbling rope that held his forelegs folded, heaved to his feet, and screamed and plunged about in a circle until the odious object crashed to the ground.

The first single file of the caravan was slowly creeping in a lengthening line across the salt flats, so very small and toy-like in that immense wasteland. Determination, plus a number of swift kicks administered by the guardian of the peace, eventually cowed our problem child into stepping along with us, sideways, bug-eyed, tense all over.

"It is only the first time," said Moulay Zeidane reassuringly.

Another string of camels detached itself from the campsite

to our left. Accompanied by the Caid, the *marabout,* Moulay
Zeidane, the guardian of the peace and a number of captives we walked across the crackling crust of the dead soil.
Two miles from the starting point everyone stopped. The
camel drivers and our little band huddled together in
separate groups, whispering, invoking the blessings of Allah.
Najim walked around our camels three times, mumbling
incantations and, after taking leave of our friends, we moved
on to join the *azalaï:* five hundred camels laden with salt.

Now there wasn't a sound in the world, except a single
voice, chanting farewell, far behind us:

"*Allah ikohoun machak.* . . . May Allah be with you. . . .
Don't lose your way. . . . May your road be safe. . . ."

It was a great relief to get out of that pestilential trap,
Taoudéni; to be heading south into clean open space over
the dreary salt plain to the passage of Foum Alous, a gap in
a gigantic razor-edged dune. The camels, astounded and
hesitant at the sight of the boundless desert beyond, behaved
as if they had never seen anything like it before. Up and
down the caravan files the drivers encouraged the animals to
step up their pace:

"Oh . . . oh . . . háha . . ."

We were on our way to Timbuctoo.

FOUR

SAHARA

1   Peoples and Cities of the Desert

HOWBEIT NOTWITHSTANDING AFRICA HATH FARRE GREATER EXTENSION
of ground than Europe, yet it is not so populous, nor so commodi-
ous to inhabite: for the lande is in many places unhabitable; the
principall causes whereof are, the scarcitie of water, the barren-
ness of the soile, being either couevered with unprofitable sande,
dust, or ashes, or else being subiet to extreme heate of the sunne:
also there are certaine dangerous heapes of sande, which raised by
the winde, are driuen up and down like the waues of a tempestu-

ous sea. In briefe there are such abundance of venemous and hurtfull creatures, that for feare of them the lande in some places can very hardly, and in others by no meanes be manured or inhabited.

This, in the translation of John Pory, is the opinion of Leo Africanus, a Moor baptized as Giovanni Leone, who traveled through the desert in 1513. Three hundred and fifty years later René Caillié, a Frenchman dedicated against all odds to the discovery of Timbuctoo, concurred with this observation in his journal after crossing the Sahara from the Niger to Morocco: "At the sight of this spectacle, of this horrible nudity, I forgot my sufferings for a moment, reflecting upon the violent convulsions which seemed to have laid bare part of an ocean; the sudden catastrophies that had rocked our world."

The theory that the entire Sahara is a dried-up ocean floor has been disproved. Remnants of fish and deposits of shells merely indicate that fresh-water marshes once occupied the low-lying regions. Some scholars suggested that the sand is the result of volcanic eruptions, others, that it blew across from the valley of the Nile. Some believed that the rocks, cracked by extremes of temperature, were pulverized by the action of wind and sun. Along with some of these factors, the most likely explanation is that the desert was caused by radical climatic changes. During the Ice Age, apparently, the Sahara was part of a relatively moist and temperate zone. As the ice receded northward, the soil gradually lost its moisture, rivers contributed to the disintegration and left sediments before they dried up or went underground, the winds perpetuated the erosion, the grasslands withered away, rainfall became a rare phenomenon.

The total area of the Sahara (from the Arabic *sahra*: desert) is estimated at three and a half million square miles stretching from the Atlantic Ocean to the Red Sea, from the Atlas Mountains to the Niger, here and there sinking below sea level, with temperatures during the hot season ranging from 120 to 130 degrees in the shade, and rising to heights of close to nine thousand feet in two major mountain chains: the Hoggar and the Tibesti. Only about 7 per cent of the desert is exclusively sand: the regions of the dunes called *erg*. The great rolling plains (*reg*) and the rocky plateau country (*hamada*) make up most of its surface. One of the Saharan rivers reached the sea: the Oued Draa; the others were absorbed by the desert. Of all the dry river beds that occasionally become violent torrents, the Oued Saoura alone flows regularly in the spring when the snows melt in the Atlas Mountains. Fossils, vestiges of petrified forests, rock engravings of animals bear witness to an earlier existence of vegetation and wild life, and areas totally sterile today abound in stone relics of prehistoric inhabitants.

Petroglyphs are found throughout northern Africa. It is believed that they were made by a Negro people about twenty thousand years ago. They are very similar to the ones found in the caves of southern Europe, and closely resemble those of the African bushmen. All this is a mystery. The only indigenous North African people about which we know anything are the Berbers, a white "Mediterranean" race. They were there long before the Arabs appeared; never a nation, never a unified people, but many factions

Peoples and Cities of the Desert · *103*

with the same racial background (probably Egyptian) related by a common Hamitic language.

Phoenicians, Greeks, Romans, Vandals plundered or colonized parts of North Africa. From the seventh to the eleventh centuries the Arabs swept into the Maghreb, the northern coastline, with the sword, the faith of Islam, and the camel.

The first Arab invasion was a planned military occupation of key points; later, a tidal wave of murderous Bedouins flooded North Africa. These Bedouins, principally the tribe of the Beni Hillal, who had come to the Maghreb from northern Arabia via Egypt, put an end to Roman colonization. The Moroccan Berbers not only survived their bloody depredations but, a hundred years after the first onslaught, roundly trounced them in two battles under the leadership of their sultan, Abd el Moumen, who banished all the captured women and children of the Beni Hillal from the eastern Maghreb to Marrakech and then invited the defeated Arab chieftains to come and claim them.

The Moroccan Berbers, living farthest away to the west from the point of impact of the Arab invasion, were not as severely affected by it as the tribes to the east. It was the coalescence of the Berbers with the Arabs that made possible the conquest of Spain, but it was also the smoldering hatred between the two peoples which contributed to the gradual weakening of their competitive administration and the final collapse of their hold on the Iberian peninsula.

There are marked differences between Berbers and Arabs apart from language. Arabs are inclined to be lazy and fanatically religious; they will blindly follow an autocratic leader. Berbers generally are industrious, skeptical about religion, and essentially democratic. The Kabyles, for example, have what is perhaps the only infallible political system: vote by unanimity.

Today, among the inextricable confusion of Arabized Berbers and Berberized Arabs, certain factions of the original stock have remained surprisingly pure. This is true of the Berbers in Morocco, the Kabyles in the Algerian Atlas Mountains, the Mozabites of Ghardïa, The Tuareg of the Hoggar.

Among the great Arab nomads, the Chaamba were masters of all the central Algerian desert between the western and the eastern dunes, and from the oasis of Ouargla in the north to the Tidikelt region below In-Salah in the south. They proudly call themselves Habb el Reeh, Breath of the Wind. Early in the conquest, the Chaamba aligned themselves with the French and furnished the most reliable guides and the finest desert fighters during the occupation of the Sahara. Their worst enemies have always been the Tuareg.

In the southern desert, adjoining the Niger River, the Berabish and the Kounta remain strong, though less martial, Arab tribes. The western desert is the country of the "Moors," Mauritania, of which the northern region into Spanish Río de Oro is the dominion of the fearless Reguibat, the Apaches of the Sahara.

Though outlaws, they never were ruffians in our sense. They were cruel, certainly; they lived in a cruel world and their Prophet had condoned the sword. They did not love their neighbor as they did themselves; nor were they hypocritical about it. Like the Tuareg, they had an evil reputation for attacking in the dark which, nowadays, is common practice. Moreover, no man was pressed into fighting against his will. There were warriors, by choice, and *marabouts* (engaged in trading and stock-raising in addition to their religious functions) who did not bear arms. Quite frequently, the warriors would steal from the *marabouts,* who, on principle, did not resist, but later sent a delegation to the culprits which, usually, succeeded in bringing back most of the loot.

Long-range raids were carefully planned and highly organized according to an accepted tradition. A rich man, or chieftain, furnished camels and arms to the warriors who volunteered for a raid. At the successful conclusion of a venture, he conceded half the take to those who returned. Participation in a raid demanded great skill and incredible endurance; the gain was much harder to come by than that, say, of the degenerate young Arab pimps of Boulevard Clichy who have assimilated Western culture to the extent of zoot suits, booze, pinball machines, and, since our last war, a few American four-letter words.

The change from the African elephant of the Carthaginians to the use of Arabian camels was equivalent to an economic revolution in that it made possible a caravan trade across vast territories which had been impassable before. There is often no transition in Oriental chronicles from rational observations to rivers of precious stones and cities of gold and silver. Many of the places mentioned by early Arab travelers existed, but no one will ever know the truth about these ancient cities, half legendary, nearly forgotten, most of them vanished. Ghana and Aoudaghost, whose locations are unknown, once were thriving markets in the southwestern Sahara. To the north, in Morocco, the ruins of Sijilmassa (a town which dates back to around A.D. 760) can be traced over a distance of five miles. Sijilmassa was visited by the geographer Ibn Haukal, and a tenth century historian, Al-Muquadasi, speaks of it as "an important town at a short distance from a river. It is both hot and cold, and the climate is healthy. The city is well supplied with dates, fresh and dried grapes, fruits, cereals and other agricultural products. It is an important market place and attracts many strangers. The inhabitants are Sunnites: good and intelligent people. There are silver mines at Tazrart and, between this district and the Land of the Blacks, mines of the purest gold in the world. The roads to Sijilmassa are difficult and lead across savage deserts."

Dogs fattened on dates were sold as a choice item in the market. Much of the merchandise in Sijilmassa was brought by caravans from Tlemcen, another important trading center in the north which, in turn, received goods through the ports of Honain and Tangier. Fine Spanish silks came from Almería, and cowrie shells, widely used as currency in the interior, were imported from the coast of East Africa.

In contrast to the marauding tribesmen who terrorized the caravan routes, the merchants of these trading centers were scrupulously honest. All transactions were carried out according to established rules and standard measures. From Sijilmassa, caravans laden with goods from Europe, Morocco and Tafilelt traveled along the Oued Saoura south across the desert to Ghana and Aoudaghost, and later to Oulata, usually taking from two to three months. A road to the west led to Ouadan in Mauritania, and from there to Río de Oro. A more easterly route passed through Tabelbala and Touat to Araouan and Timbuctoo.

Ghana, according to Ibn Haukal, was ten to twenty days' march east of Aoudaghost—which is of no help to us. It is said to have been administered by a long line of white princes, possibly Syrian Jews, before the Berbers conquered the area under a Venaga chief named Tiloutane who instituted a profitable protection racket for the safeguarding of caravans. In 1240, Ghana was destroyed by the Malinkes whose realm, the powerful Mali empire, lasted from the eighth through the fourteenth centuries and extended at its height all the way from the Senegal River in the west to the northern provinces of modern Nigeria in the east. Ghana was one of the most prominent gold and slave markets in West Africa for nearly a thousand years; Aoudaghost barely lasted one hundred. Even so, it became famous throughout the Sahara for its beautiful and obliging women and for the culinary accomplishments of the native cooks who excelled in such delicate dishes as grilled camel garnished with truffles, marcaroni soaked in honey, and snakes cooked in absinthe.

By 1300, Oualata had superseded Ghana and Aoudaghost as a commercial center. "Caravans arrived in Oualata from every country," states the Tarikh es-Sudan, "and rich men, scholars and pious personages of all races came to establish themselves in the city." But the prosperity of Timbuctoo—which had become the clearinghouse for the western desert of the trade from Djenné—was the ruin of Oualata. Although subjected to ninety-nine sieges, Djenné remained unconquered during the thirteenth and fourteenth centuries and retained its commercial importance by accepting Islam and paying tribute to the Mali empire. It was sacked subsequently by the Mossi, Songhaï and Moroccans but, despite centuries of political intrigue and civil wars of utmost cruelty, its trade continued and the city and its civilization are remarkably intact to this day.

"Djenné is one of the great markets of the Moslem world," says Es-Sadi in the Tarikh. "There the merchants who deal in salt from Teghaza meet those who bring gold from the mines of Bitou. Everyone finds it profitable to do business, and fortunes are made of which only God—be He praised! —knows the extent."

2 Caravan Routes and the Slave Trade

CARAVANS FREQUENTLY HAD TO REVISE THEIR ITINERARY depending on permits or refusals of passage through nomad territories, or because of raiding parties or tribal wars. The longest and most difficult route always was the safest; the shorter routes, relatively well supplied with water, were constantly exposed to attack. Hence the safest way from Morocco to the Niger was not the direct route from Tafilelt to the Sudan, but the roundabout road from Oued Noun to Seguiet el Hamra and Ouadan to Senegal, and from there via Tichit and Araouan to Timbuctoo. A dangerous trail through the central desert led from the oases of the Touat through the Hoggar to In Zize (a water point with an extinct volcano as a landmark), and from there south to the Niger.

The ancient salt trail from Teghaza to Oualata switched in the sixteenth century to that from Taoudéni to Timbuctoo. The earliest of all desert routes was the Tripoli-Fezzan trail mentioned by Herodotus. The prolonged trans-Saharan roads from Ghadames and Ghat to Gao via Aïr and Adrar were never safe from raiding Tuareg, and neither was the slave and ivory trail from Kano and Katsina in the Hausa country via Tassaoua, Iferouan and Ghat which supplied the markets of Tunis, Tripoli, Benghasi. For protection, Ghadamese merchants traveling south joined the annual caravan from Bilma which carried salt to the eastern desert and the region of Lake Chad. With indispensable halts, the trek from Ghadames to Kano took three months. The market of Kukawa, southwest of Lake Chad, became the terminal point for caravans to Bornu. Later traffic was directed due north from Bornu through Kaouar and Tibesti to Mourzouk.

The route along the left bank of the Niger from Kano via Sokoto to Timbuctoo, though convenient and direct, was a death trap most of the time because of the Tuareg.

In the north, the camel trails of the Chaamba and the nomads of the Tidikelt led from In-Salah to Ghadames, and to Ouargla and Gabès, the latter an oasis in Tunisia. The transverse routes of caravans carrying pilgrims toward Mecca, which started from Fez, either went by way of Laghouat, Biskra and Tozeur to Gabès; or via In-Salah, Ghadames, Aoujelah to Cairo and Alexandria.

The Libyan desert has remained the most difficult obstacle to caravans ever since the army of Cambyses set out from Thebes to conquer Ammon (the modern oasis of Siwah) and was never heard of again. In the early nineteenth century several caravans perished in attempting to connect Benghasi via Koufra with Ouadaï and Darfur.

In view of all the extremes of the desert, it is characteristic that some of the caravan centers lasted well over a thousand years while others were ravaged and disappeared overnight. Perhaps it is because they never knew if a certain place would be there on arrival, or the one they had left behind still exist upon their return, that camel drivers acquired the cautious habit of referring merely to regions. They don't say that they started from In-Salah to go to Zinder, but that they left the Touat in the hope of reaching Damerghou.

Agades is a case in point. As a storage place for the trade from Gao, it was a prosperous city of about thirty thousand. When the Tuareg pillaged Gao in 1790, Agades was left high and dry, and most of the inhabitants packed up and emigrated to the Hausa cities farther south.

The Tuareg always were a terrible menace to the desert trade, but they also were the best of all camel men and caravan guides and rendered invaluable service when they were so inclined by their thorough knowledge of pastures and waterholes. If they taxed caravans to the hilt for crossing their territory, it was better to satisfy their demands than to be waylaid by them. The Turkish pashas in the north and the native sultans in the south all played this holdup game.

The basic trade goods were salt, slaves, gold and ivory. To these were added such exports from Bornu and the Sudan as hides, ostrich plumes, gum arabic, cotton, senna, dried meat and fruits, incense, bees' wax, indigo, seeds, leather whips and bags, kola nuts and vegetable or shea butter (which has the unique quality of remaining unaffected by hot weather).

In exchange, the caravans from the north brought rugs and spices, silks and cloth, tobacco, paper, copper, tin, glass beads and mirrors, needles, broadswords, tea and sugar, musk, amber, coral, rose leaves and tar for lining water-skins and for the treatment of mangy camels. Hashish, guns and ammunition became remunerative sidelines.

The supplying markets profited not only by the trade goods they sold, but also by the sale of provisions for the camel men themselves who necessarily bought great quantities of rice and millet, dried meat, sugar, tea and fodder and harness for their animals.

Algiers never sent caravans directly into the interior but traded instead with intermediate markets. Some of the pilgrims combined their trips to Mecca with commercial transactions and carried along small cargoes of rugs and Moroccan slippers to trade against cotton goods and fabrics from India. Each market of any size was the center of a considerable local traffic in the products of the region, and "provision" caravans supplied the slave depots with dates of poor quality, *ghusub* (small, hard corn), mutton fat and *couscous*. Slave caravans differed from strictly commercial camel trains in that they carried mainly food and water, and possibly some lightweight merchandise like ostrich plumes.

Slaves were the greatest incitement for camel men to risk

the hardships and the dangers of a trans-Saharan trek. Before Cairo was built, and until the Portuguese established "factories" on the west coast of Africa in 1492, the slave trade had been an overland traffic exclusively in the hands of Moslems and pagan kings. Now Europeans bolstered the inland trade by demanding slaves for shipment up the coast of Spain and later directly to Brazil and the West Indies where Negroes had to be substituted for the Indians who had been slaughtered or worked to death in the mines. By the middle of the sixteenth century, Lisbon had become a busy shipping center of human cargoes to the New World with twice the turnover of such African markets as Kano. When French, Dutch, Danish and British factories sprung up along the coast, diplomats gravely set up official boundaries for slave pens under the jurisdiction of the various nationalities to assure the smooth functioning of the trade and to avoid unpleasantness among the representatives.

It was ticklish business dealing in such perishable merchandise, but the traders could easily afford the normal loss of 50 per cent in transit from the inland stations to the coast, and all was well if half of an Atlantic cargo reached the auction blocks of the West Indies and America.

The native merchants, whose principal markets had been in the Moslem countries, were delighted with these new outlets. Sometimes they managed to cash in both ways, black and white. In front of the opera house in Algiers are two commemorative tablets, which read:

In memory of Miguel Cervantes Saavedra, held captive in Algiers from 1575 to 1580.

Caravan Routes and the Slave Trade · *113*

In memory of the poet Regnard, enslaved at Algiers from 1678 to 1681.

From the Mediterranean coast slaves were exported to Turkey; they were shipped to India from East Africa, and to Arabia across the Red Sea. The desert trade radiated from the depots at Djenné and Timbuctoo northward to the Touat and Morocco, and from Gao and Kano toward the markets of Ghadames, Tripoli, Cairo and Benghasi.

War was the most common method of obtaining slaves. The tribute leveled by a conqueror usually included the demand for a specified number of them. When the Arabian chieftain Uquba ben Nahfi invaded Tripoli in the year 666, he concluded a peace treaty with the people of Ouadan. Annoyed by their reluctance to comply with his terms, Uquba marched upon the town with four hundred men. He had the king brought before him and personally cut off his ear.

"Why do you treat me like this," asked the king, "when we have surrendered?"

"Because it will be a lesson to you," said Uquba. "Now, every time you try to touch your ear, you will remember that you must not let yourself be tempted to resist the Arabs."

Then Uquba imposed a fine of three hundred and sixty slaves.

On the African continent itself enormous quantities of slaves were required in the oases, especially for tunneling *foggaras*: underground channels which brought water to the desert settlements from the higher plateau country. An elaborate system of *foggaras* existed at Marrakech and, at Tabelbala, southeast of Sijilmassa, underground galleries twelve miles long were dug out by hand.

Christian Abyssinia was one of the foremost consumers, and black kings throughout East, West and Central Africa accumulated slaves not only as servants, but as a mark of prestige and for sacrificial purposes. On his pilgrimage to Mecca in 1324, Kankan-Mussa, king of Mali, crossed the African continent with a sumptuous caravan preceded by five hundred slaves carrying gold staffs.

Young black women were in great demand at all times, and although the Prophet had admonished the faithful: "Force not your slave girls to whoredom!" his command was not always followed to the letter. Women and children were allowed to mount the camels at intervals in transit; male slaves, manacled and barefooted, were forced to walk across the desert. Before they were put up for sale, the dealers fattened them at the receiving stations. Normally, a trans-Saharan caravan was composed of something like two to three hundred free men, eight to nine hundred slaves, and six hundred to a thousand camels. The Tuareg were mild in their treatment of slaves; the Tibbou camel men on the Bornu-Fezzan route had the worst reputation in Africa for cruelty. They were notorious for violating children, and for flogging and starving their slaves to death.

Ibn Batuta, the famous Arab traveler, returned from the Sudan in 1353 with a caravan of six hundred women slaves. He speaks of an Arab who had been banished by a Negro ruler to a wild region where he lived with cannibals for four years. "The reason why the heathens did not eat him, was that he was white, for they say that the white is indigestible because he is not 'ripe,' whereas the black is 'ripe' in their opinion." Ibn Batuta further relates that "Sultan Mausa Sulayman was visited by a party of these Negro cannibals, including one of their amirs. The sultan received them with honor, and gave them as his hospitality-gift a female slave. They killed and ate her, and having smeared their faces and hands with her blood, came to the sultan to thank him. I was informed that this is their regular custom whenever they visit his court. Someone told me about them that they say that he choicest parts of women's flesh are the palm of the hand and the breasts."

Many Negroes sold their children—and often themselves and their entire families—out of poverty. The natives of the Sudan and Bornu hinterland were in perpetual fear of slave-hunting expeditions sent out by the local sultans. The easy way of capturing women and children was for one tribe to swoop down upon another when the warriors of the village under attack were away pillaging a third.

The most wasteful, but also the most profitable, aspect of slavery was the trade in eunuchs. They were highly valued as guardians of harems, and frequently rose to important positions in the courts of Negro kings and Moslem rulers. The rich sultans of Bornu, Baguirmi and Kanem owned hundreds and even thousands of eunuchs. The traders in Morocco, Tripoli and Fezzan sold them at profits of from 300 to 500 per cent. Among potentates they were the ideal gift. The Tarikh es-Sudan records the visit of an envoy from Morocco to the court of Askia El-Hadj in Gao: "The prince gave the Moroccan visitor a brilliant reception and, at the moment of his departure, presented him with double the amount of gifts which he had received, such as slaves, musk, and eighty eunuchs."

The Mossi of the Upper Volta region and the natives of Mandara, south of Lake Chad, were particularly skilled in performing the delicate operation. Out of a group of children, captured young men or prisoners of war about to be put to death, candidates were carefully chosen for physical fitness; even so only ten out of a hundred could hope to survive. Al-Muquaddasi speaks of the operation as it was practiced in the tenth century:

I interviewed a group of eunuchs about the procedure of castration and learned that the Rûm [?] emasculated boys and then shut them away so as to keep them from preoccupying themselves with girls, and to spare them the tortures of carnal desires. But opinions differ on the methods of castration. One says that incisions are made in the penis and the testicles at the same time, another claims that the testicles are removed and a stem is inserted under the penis before it is split from the root up. I asked the eunuch Urayb, who is intelligent and sincere: "Tell me about the eunuchs, for the scholars don't agree about them. Abu Hanifa says that they can have wives, and that they can claim the paternity of the children which their wives bring into the world; this is a point only you can clarify."

"Abu Hanifa is right," he said, "and I will tell you how it is possible. When the operation takes place, the testicles are cut open and flattened out. Now, it may happen that the child is frightened [sic] and that one of the testicles slips upward into the abdomen; they try to get hold of it, but they don't always find it, and it comes down again when the incisions have healed. If it is the

Caravan Routes and the Slave Trade • 117

left testicle, the eunuch is capable of desire and can secrete sperm; if it is the right one, he can grow a beard. Thus, a father may well be one of those eunuchs who have kept one testicle."

After the operation a leaden shaft is placed in the urinary canal which is taken out when necessary, but which is retained there until the cure is completed so that the tissues heal without closing the orifice.

These surgical transformations could be performed in such a way that the results closely resembled female genitals. Eunuchs of this type had a particular market value.

The eventual abolition of slavery in the Americas had a disastrous effect on the West African export trade, but the traffic across the Sahara continued. James Richardson, the English explorer, took a dim view of it during his visit to the Fezzan in 1846. However, his approach to native problems must have been very tactful, for Mohammed Shafou Ben Seed, sultan of the Tuareg of Ghat, gave the matter serious thought in a letter to Her Majesty, the Queen of England:

. . . The said James opposed himself to this [the slave traffic] saying, that you mentioned to him that this trade ought to be abolished. You should therefore shew us in what manner we can do away with it. If we find you are right, we shall follow your advice; but if you are wrong, your order shall not be executed. We never flog our slaves, nor let them get hungry, and we do unto them all good.

After this, we shall send you a present, in order that you may perceive that the Touaricks are friendly to the English. We are poor, we have very little money; but you will receive a knife, which is to be tied on the arm, a spear, a shield made of bullocks' skin, and a leathern cushion, which we send, invoking the blessing of Allah.

These are very small objects, but we are poor, and the only further things we possess are camels, but we are afraid they would die on the road if we were to send them to you.

The picture of Queen Victoria with a Tuareg dagger strapped to her arm is somewhat ludricous. Her Majesty probably heaved a sigh of relief at the thought of having escaped the camels.

A good male slave bought in Kano for ten Spanish dollars was sold in Tripoli for sixty; a young female worth thirty dollars in Bornu, fetched one hundred on the northern markets.

In the middle of the nineteenth century, three-fourths of the money which supported the Saharan traffic of slaves into Arabia, Turkey and Abyssinia, was put up by European traders.

Slave hunts were carried out in Ouadaï as late as 1904, and in 1906 a French military patrol intercepted and defeated a caravan which was transporting one hundred and fifty children across the eastern Sahara toward the slave markets of Tripoli.

The trans-Saharan camel trade of the present day has dwindled to the two main salt routes: from Taoudéni to Timbuctoo in the western Sudan, and from Bilma to Agades and Zinder in the east. Tahoua and Agades are active markets for native goods. In 1927 there were seven thousand camels in the area; thanks to the help and encouragement of an intelligent administration which seriously concerned itself with the construction of desert wells, there were five times as many nine years after the French occupation. By 1946 the Kaouar *azalaï* mustered twenty-five thousand camels.

Potash and salt are carried from Magaria in the French Niger colony to Kano by camel trains often numbering a thousand animals. During the groundnut (peanut) season, these Tuareg caravans then continue to Maiduguri in the northeast corner of Nigeria to transport the accumulated stocks from there back to Kano, where the bags are stacked in enormous pyramids. Caravans also deposit great quantities of peanuts from the hinterland in Madarounfa and Maradi across the northern border of Nigeria. The strange piebald camels of this region are led by men in leather skirts which are slashed into long strips down the sides. These Negroid Tuareg are untidy and ferocious characters who never are without their swords, even when they load or unload sacks of peanuts.

Not many years ago an important dope ring was uncovered in Morocco. For a long time all attempts to detect the method of delivery failed, although the authorities knew that a considerable traffic in opium and heroin existed. Goods carried by caravans were subjected to a rigorous control; nothing objectionable could be found. The animals used by suspected smugglers carried perfectly innocent merchandise on their backs, but they had been forced to swallow metal capsules containing the drugs which thus could be transported safely in large quantities. At the point of destination the camels were butchered and the containers retrieved. It took an X-ray examination of one of the suspected caravans to put a stop to this lucrative business.

3   Caravan

MY INTRODUCTION TO THE TAOUDÉNI SALT CARAVAN HAD BEEN informal, to say the least. Being busy with our own preparations, we barely caught up with it at the last minute. It was not unusual that the departure took place so late in the day; most caravans travel a short distance at the start to allow stragglers to come up during the first halt, or to make any changes that might be necessary in the lineup of the animals or in the distribution of the loads before settling down to the regular routine of the long daily treks. We had joined the middle group of three sections; there was one ahead of us and another one behind. In the open desert they proceeded in three or four parallel files of thirty to forty animals, with a man at the head of each file. Each camel had a rope tied to its lower jaw, the other end of the rope (*arahbe*) being attached to the preceding animal's tail.

In the bright glare and the uniform emptiness around us the camels stamped their tracks upon the diagonal pattern of terra-cotta sand. Most of them carried four bars of salt, a few of the strongest ones five, the smaller ones two, and the novices to the hard life on the trail swayed along with a light ballast of broken pieces on their backs. Provisions, water skins, sleeping mats and cooking utensils were distributed among the lot. The animals, both male and female, varied in age from six to twenty-one.

A young camel is classified by a specific name each year according to his age. At the age of one he is called *ben ashar,* at two *belboun,* at three *henk,* at four *jda,* at five *f'ni,* at six *erbah.* At the age of seven he loses these distinctions and becomes a plain *djemel.*

Najim's mount had, but did not respond to, the name Lassfar, the Yellow One, docile due to age and desperation. Our good pack camel, a dirty brown in color, was Lachmar, the Red One, honest but indifferent. My resigned female, with a large oozing cyst on her right upper lid, was Albéwua, the White One, long-suffering and philosophical in choosing the path of least resistance. The nasty little fellow who hated the wooden box, frightened but willing, was Lachlar, the Blue One, although there wasn't a trace of blue in him. All the camels of the caravan had names in addition to those designating age, unflattering ones among them. The outstanding lead camel was Towshee (so called after his owner), an exceptionally intelligent animal, the only one that took an interest in what went on around him when all the others plodded along in a coma. Towshee, at the head of his file, led a whole string of lesser camels without guidance. He probably knew the trail better than anyone and followed his impertinent nose with complete confidence. No doubt he also knew a good deal about camels.

In ideal conditions (practically nonexistent in the Sahara) a loaded pack camel can cover about three miles and a half per hour, the nature of the ground and the state of the weather being often more decisive in the progress of the caravan than the speed and endurance of the animals. During the cool season, a caravan travels from four in the morning until evening; in the hot season, the men prefer to march through the night and to rest during the day. Some of the merchants supply their own camels, others hire large numbers of them from the Tuareg; the Moorish drivers themselves use all suitable animals from the herds in their encampments.

After walking for two hours we mounted and rode beside the *aghab el moghdar*, the rear guard of the caravan, who keeps a constant watch on the animals ahead of him. The shorter the files, the more convenient it is for him to supervise them for, in addition to following the trail, he has to run up and down the line whenever a load needs readjusting or a rope slips off an animal's tail. When a link is broken, the separated string of camels will either stop or wander away or get all tied up in knots.

Deeah, the rear guard, answered my greeting with a courtly little bow.

The only landmarks were bleached bones and, camels being very apt to shy at skeletons, Najim warned me to hold on to the saddle and to pull my camel's head back tightly when our animals were frightened by a carcass. His candid opinion was that camels are good animals, but that no one can trust them because, when you least expect it, they turn out to be very nasty brutes.

To ride a caravan camel seems excruciatingly slow; to walk beside one is too fast for comfort. There was hardly any evidence of men among so many camels, the ratio being six to one hundred. Some of the drivers marched along with well-co-ordinated movements, others kept up a half-running coolie shuffle; all of them showed a perfect sense of balance in maneuvering about on a pack animal in motion once they had clambered aboard by grabbing a shoulder and one ear, swinging one knee into the crook of the camel's neck and inching up the narrow slope to the top. Two bandy-legged drivers marched briskly side by side halfway up the column, several others walked with their *karouass,* the camel club, braced across their necks; a teen-aged boy, on his first voyage, went running along on nimble feet, and Salah, our *amenir,* the guide and master of the camel train, strode forward at the head of the caravan like the conqueror of the world.

Their flimsy garments and their lamentable footgear seemed inadequate for such an arduous journey, yet long tradition and experience had proved the value of their short and baggy trousers, the loose *reshahba* (a knee-length shirt) gathered at the waist by a broad belt, their leather sandals with the square sole turned back over the toes, and the dark-blue headcloth.

The sun was full out but a cold wind blew from the north; we were baked in front and chilled in the back: typical Saharan pneumonia weather for early December.

The saddles used in the western Sahara are of the Mauritanian type in contrast to the Tuareg saddle. The latter is light in weight with a small circular seat, a high pommel in the form of a cross, and a flat pointed board in the back.

Tuareg camels are trained to hold their heads high so that the rider may conveniently place his bare feet on the arched neck. This is the only position the Tuareg seat permits. The Moorish saddle—*rahla,* pronounced *rahchla,* literally "departure"—is designed for animals with outstretched necks. It is heavier and constructed along the lines of a bucket seat which flares upward, butterfly-fashion, around the sides and in the rear, with a low flat pommel in front. The Mauritanian saddle demands a style of riding entirely different from that of the Tuareg. In order to mount a couched Moorish camel, the rider pulls the rein up short and steps on it to hold the animal's head; taking hold of the pommel with his right hand, he steps up on the camel's folded foreleg; his right foot is placed on the animal's back directly in front of the saddle as his right hand switches its hold to the off-wing of the seat; rising on his right leg and performing a quarter turn, the rider eases himself into the saddle, which is more comfortable than the Tuareg seat in that it permits the rider to cross his legs on the left or on the right of the camel's shoulders, or let them relax astride on both sides. These possible variations are an advantage on long trips as they avoid the cramps that may occur after many hours in the more rigid position imposed by the Tuareg seat. However, such sweet terms as ease and comfort are strictly relative in reference to any camel saddle. The only padding is a sheepskin which is thrown over the leather-covered wooden frame. A well-trained camel should understand without urging that it is expected, when mounted, to get to its feet. Najim's camel was prevented from doing so at times by a bad case of rheumatism which allowed the poor creature to raise its rear end up in the air but kept the crippled fore-legs glued to the ground.

On this first short day we stopped at sundown. Working in pairs, the drivers relieved the snarling animals of their loads, propped the salt slabs in a long line over the desert and couched the camels in a row, tying their forelegs at the knee. Then they anchored iron tripods over little fires to cook a mess of rice and jerky. They were all very dark, made of muscle and sinew; tireless on the march and energetic at work; indolent and quiet in repose, yet instantly ready for action. Salah, our *amenir,* with his hawk nose and high cheekbones, had the face of an apostle. He could neither read nor write; he had never heard of Copernicus, but this illiterate individual was the wisest member of the party; without him we would soon be lost.

We ate in silence, stacked our baggage against the wind and shivered through the night beside the moaning, belching camels. In the bitter cold at three o'clock next morning we were on our way again. Time and the desert before us seemed endless. In the first light of day we passed a solitary cone, Ghelb el Abid, the Heart of the Captive. Here a slave who had escaped from Taoundéni had died of thirst. It is characteristic of the Arabs to witness, or contribute to, a tragedy and then to find a poetic name for it.

For many hours the caravan wound through a region of rolling dunes. None of the camel drivers spoke a word of French. They knew about Mecca but had no idea of Arabia; they were completely ignorant about Europe and had never heard of Egypt or the Nile. Nonetheless, they were intelligent within their sphere, and Najim was particularly alert in his, but in the company of the camel men, absorbed by trifling gossip and heroic nonsense, a curious transformation took place. He who had been so honeyvoiced and so solicitous, so anxious "to do everything for you and tell you all you want to know," the slightly stoopshouldered Najim with the small hands and quick gestures and the skin the color of a smoked oyster who had formerly offered me my glass of tea inside of a covered saucepan to keep the flies from drowning in it, this same Najim now had long periods of mental blankness during which our verbal contact dropped to zero. He had conveyed to me more than once that he was a brilliant conversationalist in Songhaï, Arabic and Tamachec, but suddenly he was peculiarly resistant to the use and meaning of the "language of France." To me, on the other hand, it was much more of a strain to speak Arabic than French.

I ventured to remark: "I imagine the camel drivers are surprised to see me."

"What?"

It was very difficult to get his attention. The question was blown right back at me by the wind.

"I say, I suppose the people of the caravan are surprised that I want to travel with them."

"The people?"

"Yes."

"Now?"

"Yes, our camel drivers."

"Our camel drivers? What about them?"

"I say they must be surprised to see me."

"See you? Where?"

"Here, among them."

"Oh, the people of the caravan? No, they knew you were coming before we got started."

Well, so much for that. They didn't show any surprise, certainly, nor any superficial curiosity. Bani, an Arab salt merchant, who had spent several months in Taoudéni and was now returning to his home in Araouan, hobbled and skipped along beside us in a dilapidated pair of Turkish slippers of which one sole flapper loosely at each step, forever mumbling *Allahis, Bismillahs* and *Hamdullahs* to himself. He paid not the slightest attention to our enlightening conversation.

For hours on end the caravan proceeded without a sound, no more sound, at any rate, than the almost inaudible tread of the camels, the chafing of two salt bars or the creaking of a cord: a silent procession in a land without echo, the only movement in a world of immobility. But the movement was so slow and we had so far to go that our progress seemed to be illusory and our effort hopeless in that we appeared to be walking on an endless belt, forever slipping away from under us, against a stationary backdrop of monumental emptiness. Weakened in the midday heat by physical exertion during these long and uneventful passages, one's body succumbed to a painful lassitude, the mind became numb the eyes were blurred by the quivering ground and by the dragging gait of the camels as they put each hind foot down a fraction of a second before each front foot, first on one side, then on the other, as if two independent camel-halves had been joined together to achieve a method of propulsion contrary to other animals.

Our daily routine was to walk for three hours in the morning, to ride for four hours in the middle of the day, to walk another three hours toward evening and to mount again until we stopped for the night. While walking, very little was said; it was the languor of the camels' stride and the relief from having to watch the stones underfoot that encouraged conversation when we were mounted.

The bland panorama took on a new aspect as a slightly darker streak on the horizon enriched the view ahead of us.

"Krenachich," said Najim. "That is where we will camp tonight."

Bani perched like a gargoyle on top of his bleary-eyed beast among his belongings: sacks and garments and two gallons of goat butter, arranged so that he could crouch in the middle of it all behind the hump.

We had not stopped once since early morning. The camel drivers had scooped a few handfuls of millet out of their bags, had kneaded it into a thick liquid with a little water in their wooden bowls and tossed it off on the run. Now we were traveling much more slowly in one long line along a rocky path in the darkness. The men soothed the nervous animals with soft calls as we twisted and turned uphill and down.

"Hoh ... eeeh...! Hoh ... eeeh!"

It was nine-thirty before we came to the waterholes of Krenachich where the caravan spread out and came to rest in a wide basin at the foot of a stony ridge. Part of the valley was occupied by the preceding camel train and shadowy figures moved about in the light of the campfires.

Each caravan on the northward trek cut and gathered

Caravan · *129*

fodder where it was available and then left piles of it at strategic points which served to feed the animals on the return trip from the mines. As soon as our camels were unloaded—a hard job after twenty hours on the trail—the drivers spread their stored provender of *shot* (a long, dry grass) among the hungry beasts. The night was so cold that we had four glasses of tea after the manner of the Reguibat instead of the customary three. When the rice had cooked to a pulp we ate it gratefully and, desperately tired, bundled up to sleep.

All the ancient camel trails of the western route to Timbuctoo converge upon the waterholes of Krenachich, an escarpment of black rock divided by ravines which permit passage to the plateau above.

The water of Krenachich is famous far and wide for its delightful purity, but many of the old waterholes were sanded up; the three in current use were dirty puddles at the bottom of sloping pits ten feet deep. The water was full of sediment, to put it mildly, and blood-red.

Since the year 1000, long before salt was hauled from Taoudéni to the Sudanese markets, men and beasts traveling down from Teghaza, and from Tatental before that, "filled their veins," as the nomads say, at the waterholes of Krenachich. During the halts, the caravans posted lookouts on the edge of the escarpment, but through the centuries until modern times marauders swooped out of the black hills into the barren valley to kill and plunder.

Salah had decided to let the camels rest here for a day and to allow everyone time to replenish the goatskins for the waterless twelve-day stretch ahead. He had killed a scorpion on his mat on rising in the morning.

"If he gets away after biting you," he said, "you will be very sick, but if you kill him, the bite won't hurt you."

Mohamed Mokhtar, the oldest guide on the Timbuctoo trail, who traveled with the section ahead of us, came to our fire. He showed me a badly-healed bullet wound in his hip: a souvenir of the great battle between Berabish camel men and Reguibat raiders which took place in 1925. Mohamed related that, when he was camped again at Krenachich in 1936, he witnessed the return of the remnants of a caravan that had been lost. The survivors had subsisted for a week on the blood of their camels and on the stinking liquid in their stomachs.

The breastworks put up by the defenders of the waterholes still dotted the rocky ledge around the campsite. They were actively used until 1940, the last year in which the *azalaï* was guarded by a military escort. As I stood looking over the encampment below, I was startled by an explosive movement beside me on the ground. A large lizard, a crested baby dragon two feet long, rushed between my legs, swerved, turned again with such speed that he fell over, leaped and dashed into a hole. To claim that the desert is safe is like saying that crime has been abolished in Chicago. The camel drivers were disappointed that I had not killed the reptile. They are very fond of eating it. No wonder they don't get along with the Tuareg who never harm it, because they recognize and venerate this monster as their "uncle."

Najim and Laazize sat in the sand, surrounded by the debris of defunct camels and sun-scorched caravan equipment which had accumulated through the centuries all over this historic resting place. They were having a fine time together smoking a little pipe the size and shape of a cigarette holder, passing it back and forth for the few puffs of tobacco it contained. The pipe (*la'aloum*), a grooved steel bangle, a flint, and a dry mossy substance used as tinder were carried on a string of camel gut around the neck in a decorated oblong leather satchel, of which the outer cover slipped upward on the string, exposing an inside container with a compartment for each one of these indispensable articles, including a pair of tweezers.

When he had finished smoking, Laazize gave himself a medical treatment with hot goat butter. He suffered from a complaint very common among camel men: *sheggoug,* deep cracks in the hard, dried soles of their feet.

Before the caravan departed from Krenachich, the heavy vehicles of the desert patrol came wallowing through the sand. Each of the five cars was driven by a French officer, rows of goggled Senegalese sat behind. They drew up in parallel order; one of the cars drove over to our camp. I was invited to lunch with the officers, who received me with unstinted cordiality.

They asked me how I felt about camels by now. How I liked my companions. Did I think I could take it all the way to Timbuctoo? Did I realize that we still had a long way to go?

We had a fine stew, wine, biscuits and jam. They asked me if I had a snake-bite kit and insisted that I take one of their hypodermic needles and a set of antivenom bulbs.

"This is how you assemble the parts." One of the officers

demonstrated. "Actually, you have to make a fire and heat some water to sterilize the needle first; otherwise you might get an infection. Then you break one of the bulbs, like this. Then you fill the hypodermic up to here. When that's done, you push the plunger once to see if it works, and also to get the air out. Because if you pump air into a vein, you're sunk. Then you pinch your stomach, like this—see?—and give yourself the first shot. Don't get panicky. The next one you put in the thigh, on the outside, never on the inside! Danger of paralysis. The last one you give yourself just above the bite. Of course, sometimes you are dead before the job is finished."

When I took my leave, they gave me several packages of Goldflake cigarettes, a box of matches, a can of instant coffee. Then they asked to take my picture. This, I thought, had rather a grim connotation. Something for the family album to show to their children in the years to come. A souvenir of the crazy foreigner who had come a cropper in the Sahara. Nice enough fellow, but, *mon Dieu* . . . these Americans who think they can do anything that comes into their heads. . . . Yes, we were the last to see him. . . .

This wasn't really a joke. I wasn't imagining things, either. Many a man never had been seen again. This was no plush safari with "personal boys," hot baths and iced martinis. I was an uninvited guest among a band of hardened and very frugal camel drivers. I was getting a taste of what the early explorers had gone through. Many of those courageous men had never reached their goal, and about half of those who started out failed to return.

4   *Early Explorers*

THE EARLIEST EXPLORERS OF THE SAHARA WHO "MADE NEWS" were a group of Nasamonians, a people who inhabited part of what is now Tripoli. Herodotus briefly relates that five adventurous young men set out across Libya, and that they entered a region of wild beasts. They crossed this dangerous country unharmed, and came to a desert of sand. After a journey of many days, they found themselves in a plain of trees and fruits where they were made prisoners by little black men who led them through a labyrinth of lakes and marshes to a city traversed by a large stream.

The later Arab traveler, Ibn Battuta, is more explicit about his journey. In 1352, he left Fez—"Where running water and nourishing food are never exhausted"— and crossed the desert to the "Nile" (meaning Niger) and the kingdom of Mali which "cannot be visited by any white man because they would kill him before he got there." There was "no visible road or track in these parts, nothing but sand blown hither and thither by the wind." At Oualata he was truly amazed to find that "the men show no signs of jealousy whatever" and that "the women there have *friends* and *companions*, and the men in the same way have *companions* amongst the women of other families. A man may go into his house and find his wife entertaining her *companion* but he takes no objection to it." He also observed that "the negroes use salt as a medium of exchange, just as gold and silver is used elsewhere." Ibn Battuta was well received in Timbuctoo and speaks of Gawgaw (as the present town of Gao was then called) as "a large city on the 'Nile,' and one of the finest towns in the Negrolands." On his way north he traveled with a caravan through "the country of the Haggar, who are a tribe of Berbers; they wear face veils and are a rascally lot."

Long after mariners had conquered the seas, the Sahara remained a mystery to Europeans. The earliest concrete information about the interior was furnished by Jewish cartographers in Majorca, thanks to the knowledge they had acquired in their intercourse with Jewish colonizers and traders in Africa. A map designed by Mecia de Viladestes in 1413 indicates the Hoggar, Gao, Timbuctoo and Mali. But as if in reprisal for giving out secrets and opening up a flourishing trade, the Jews were persecuted by the Arabs toward the end of the century and crushed by massacres that spread from Spain across the desert into the Sudan.

A few Genoese traded with the Niger countries through the fourteenth and fifthteenth centuries, but our knowledge of the Sahara was very vague until a little over a hundred years ago when Europeans first reached Timbuctoo, and the wild speculations over the course of the Niger were finally settled.

The largest unknown areas left in Africa were sections of the Sahara. The oases of Arkenouh and El Aouïnat, south of Koufra, were discovered in 1922. Parts of Río de Oro, Mauritania and the Libyan desert are still unexplored.

Throughout the eighteenth century, very little interest had been shown in the interior of Africa by European nations. They were occupied by warfare and the competition for footholds and richer spoils in the Far East. The Sahara was nothing more than a blank spot on the map. The existence of the Niger at the far end of the desert was known since antiquity, but it was consistently confused with the Nile, and even in modern times there were many heated controversies among armchair geographers who have supposed, in turn, that its course lay westward, that it was a confluent of the Nile, that it could not possibly end in the Atlantic as there was no evidence of its mouth (as far as the coast was known); that it was identical with the Senegal River, that it clearly evaporated somewhere. The natives of the interior held fast to their belief that "it flows to the end of the earth."

A concerted effort toward exploration was made by the African Association which was formed in London in 1788. Its purpose was to encourage and finance missions of discovery for the sake of knowledge, the extension of commerce, and the abolition of the slave trade. There was little evidence of political motives.

Of the three original emissaries, John Ledyard, an American, succumbed to fever in Egypt before he got started; William Lucas, whose career had ranged from that of a slave in Morocco to British vice-consul, had to turn back because of wars in Tripoli; Major Daniel Houghton, who attempted to reach the desert via Gambia, was assassinated.

In 1798 a German, Friedrich Hornemann, joined a caravan in Cairo in the disguise of a Moslem after taking the precaution of having himself circumcised. In the company of a friend, Freudenberg, he succeeded in reaching Mourzouk. There Freudenberg died of fever, and the caravan, which had continued without them, was destroyed by raiding Tuareg. Hornemann returned to Tripoli and set out again for Mourzouk, and on this second voyage reached the Niger, where he died: the first European to cross the Sahara.

The African Association next sent out a brave and persevering Scotsman, Mungo Park, "regularly educated in the medical line, sufficiently instructed in the use of Hadley's quadrant to make the necessary observations; geographer enough to trace his path through the wilderness, and not unacquainted with natural history."

Unfortunately, all of this was not enough. Mungo Park perished on his second expedition into the Sudan after reporting in his last message: "I am sorry to say that of forty-five Europeans who left the Gambia in perfect health, five only are at present alive, viz. three soldiers (one deranged in his mind) Lieutenant Martyn and myself."

Major Gordon Laing, another Scotsman who had held a government post in Sierra Leone on the West African coast, attempted to solve the riddle of the Niger in 1825. He spent a year in crossing the desert from Tripoli to Timbuctoo, where he was murdered. He had made no concessions for his safety and traveled openly as a Christian in European clothes, presenting himself as an envoy of the King of England. When the Moslems tried to bully him into confessing that there was only one god, Allah, he repeated after them that there was, indeed, only one god—without specifying which one. He freely took notes on the asumption that honesty is the best policy, but it did not work. The natives later explained that he did not wish to

Early Explorers · *137*

associate with them or eat their food, and that he was not in the least "amusing."

In 1828, a poor but intrepid young Frenchman, without any financial backing, René Caillié, did return from the legendary city of Timbuctoo after incredible sufferings on his northward trek across the Sahara with a Moorish caravan. He passed himself off as an Arab born in Alexandria who had been taken as a child to Europe and subsequently to the Sudan. As an explanation for undertaking such a hazardous journey, he firmly stuck to his story of wanting to return to his kin and his Moslem brethren in Egypt. The natives were not always convinced of his innocent intentions; they suspected him of being a Christian and starved him, threw stones at him, and taunted him with crass insults. Upon his return to France, he was accused of being a fraud though, eventually, he was given the Legion of Honor and a small pension.

The British government now subsidized several expeditions for what was then known as "the Niger Quest" under the leadership of such competent explorers as Major Dixon Denham, Dr. Walter Oudney, and Lieutenant Hugh Clapperton. They carried out extensive exploration in Bornu and the Sudan, but Oudney and Clapperton died, and Denham returned to Tripoli. It was on a second voyage that Richard Lander, Clapperton's servant, finally solved the mystery of the course of the elusive river.

Interested in the possibility of new markets, the British government then sent out James Richardson to see if the Saharan slave trade could not be converted into a more respectable kind of business along British lines. As his companions, Richardson chose two distinguished German scientists, Dr. Adolph Overweg and Dr. Heinrich Barth. Richardson and Overweg died after crossing the desert, but Heinrich Barth returned after five years of the most thorough exploration of the Sahara that had yet been attempted. He was the third European to enter Timbuctoo, and the first to dispel all doubt about René Caillié's accomplishment twenty-five years earlier.

Among the later explorers of the century were men like the eminent French anthropologist Henry Duveyrier, who compiled the classic work on the Tuareg of the north; Gustav Nachtigal, who first visited the Tibesti region—and established a record by carting across the Sahara eight camel loads of gifts from the King of Prussia to the Sultan of Bornu, including a crimson throne and a harmonium; the fastidious Oskar Lenz, the first to travel the route from Morocco to Timbuctoo, where he was well received, perhaps because he won the natives by his unassuming attitude, his good chess, and his extravagant habit of sleeping between white sheets.

In 1830, French troops had landed on the beach of Sidi-Ferruch, defeated the Dey of Algiers, Hussein Pasha, and put an end to piracy. This was the beginning of the long struggle against Abd-el-Kader and the conquest of northern Algeria. The Berber tribesmen in the mountains of Kabylia held out for another thirty years. Military control over the Sahara slowly got under way. At the same time, resistance stiffened among the nomads of the interior against the penetration of their desert, which a wave of assassinations had rendered more treacherous than ever.

The possession of Algeria made an overland connection with the Sudan desirable. What better solution than a railroad across the Sahara? In Paris, the idea caught on fire. Detailed plans were made on the drawing tables, and investors clamored to get rid of their money. The Trans-Saharan Corporation sent out expeditions to study the proposed route—as far as El-Goléa. In 1880, the commission decided to explore the southern end of the line. Colonel Paul François Flatters was chosen to head an expedition of five officers, four technical experts and eighty natives, among them a detachment of the formidable Chaamba. At Temassinin, the present Fort Flatters, he learned that one of the powerful Tuareg chiefs was much farther south, and the other, Duveyrier's friend and protector, in the vicinity of Ghat. Flatters sent a message to the latter, suggesting a meeting at a point halfway between Ghat and Temassinin. There, Flatters and his men waited for a few days but, seeing that their supplies were running out, they returned to their home base. When the Tuareg chief arrived, they had left.

In December of the same year, Colonel Flatters started out from Ouargla on a second expedition, composed of ten officers and engineers and seventy-eight natives, of which fifty were Algerian soldiers posing as camel drivers. Flatters planned to proceed via Amguid south into the Hoggar, and made his intentions known to Ahitaghel, the chief of the region, who replied:

Praise be to the only God!
From Sheikh Younes, known as Ahitaghel Ben Biska, from Sheikh Mohamed Oum Tegdad Eg Igatouan and Sheikh Mohamed Ben Sheikh Hedomar to Sheikh Flatters.

We have received your message, we have read and understood it; you ask us to let you pass, we will not let you pass.

You wanted to go to Ghat, you arrived at Oued el Khamalet; we neither received a letter nor a messenger from you, and you returned to your country. You have written that you wished to come to us by way of Amadghor, and you turned back.

This is better for you.

This road does not lead to us; there is a trail through Ghat, and another through Touat, Timbuctoo and the Sudan.

We live in peace and tranquility; we have neither villages nor towns, we only have dry river beds, open tents and hidden tombs.

If you want to visit us, at Amadghor or in Aheer, let us know about yourself and about the reason for your coming; we will see what we shall do about it.

The Chaamba can tell you about us; we have no commerce in our country. Send us a message by someone; we wish to know what you want.

Colonel Flatters did not heed this warning. He was determined to continue. Ahitaghel, as if to correct his unfriendly attitude, sent a conciliatory message and a number of guides. A larger party of Tuareg joined them later. Apparently, Flatters felt perfectly secure; he did not hesitate to follow the guides with four of his officers to a well, leaving the main body of his troops behind. Before he became aware of the trap, the Tuareg attacked from all sides. They killed Flatters and the officers who were with him while another contingent massacred nearly half of his troops and ran off the camels.

Five Frenchmen and fifty natives fled northward into the

desert on foot; forty days' march from the point of departure. Their scant provisions soon dwindled to nothing and more and more stragglers were left behind. One day they met a party of Tuareg who offered them dates. Those who ate them were poisoned and stumbled away into the wilderness, laughing and screaming. Farther north they were attacked again, and three of the officers were killed. The last one was murdered by his men.

Only a handful of the native soldiers, miserable human wrecks, survived and got back to Ouargla five weeks after the disaster at the well by subsisting on the corpses of their comrades.

This fiasco was such a blow that it stopped all further attempts to invade the Sahara for the next twenty years. Capable officers in the field were frustrated by administrative bungling, and countless ill-fed camels were sacrificed through mismanagement in supplying desert outposts. The brass hats in Paris had seen camels only in the zoo and could not reconcile themselves to the picture of dignified French officers in parade uniforms aboard such ridiculous beasts. It took them many years to figure out that the uniforms were ridiculous, and that the camels were their greatest asset in the desert.

England, considering the Sahara as an unprofitable headache, relinquished all claims to it.

Around 1900 a major military effort was made to "pursue the scientific exploration of the Sahara between Algeria and the Sudan" and, incidentally, to "weld together" French North, West and Equatorial Africa by sending two other expeditions up from the south, one from the Sudan, one from the Congo, with Lake Chad as the bull's-eye.

Fernand Foureau and Commander François Lamy started, as Colonel Flatters had done, from Ouargla, but with a much more impressive force: ten officers, two hundred and eighty native soldiers, four civilians, and one thousand camels.

The trek to the southern edge of the Algerian desert took three months. For all the grandiose preparations that had been made, the expedition suffered terrible hardships and an alarming number of native soldiers, rather than go on, blew their brains out. Part of the equipment and ammunition had to be abandoned en route, and Foureau noted that, "Over a period of seven days, we have lost one hundred and forty camels." When the expedition arrived in Zinder one year after its departure from Ouargla, not one of the original thousand camels had survived. In spite of all the difficulties and delays, the three armies met at Lake Chad, but here another problem presented itself.

Rabah, an ex-slave who became a successful slave trader, had terrorized the Egyptian desert region of Bahr el Ghazal until the English made it too hot for him. He had moved west with his black army, deposing native kings right and left, pillaging and killing without mercy on his far-flung forays, and dickering with the French and British in his phony capacity as Sultan of Bornu. He would permit no incursions into his territory and had wiped out several military posts.

With a sizable force at his disposal, Commander Lamy crowned his march across the Sahara with an immediate offensive against Rabah. He defeated the black tyrant, but

Lamy himself was killed during an unexpected counter-attack.

Once, in the early part of his adventurous life, Rabah had acted as guide to a beautiful and daring young lady: Alexandrine Tinne, the richest woman in the Netherlands. Miss Tinne had come to Egypt with her mother and one of her aunts and had set up house in Cairo in lavish Oriental style. She was intensely interested in the exploration of upper Egypt and deeply concerned about the suppression of the slave trade. After two previous expeditions into regions never before visited by Europeans, she organized a third party in 1863 which took her far up the course of the White Nile through unknown swamps and deserts six hundred miles to the south of Omdurman. On this fateful voyage her mother, her aunt, one of the two scientists who accompanied her, the Italian interpreter and her two European maids, all died of fever and exhaustion, but Miss Tinne lived through the horrors of the trip and returned to Cairo with much valuable geographical information.

Six years later, undaunted by the high price she had paid for her disastrous expedition into the Egyptian Sudan, she decided to cross the Sahara to Timbuctoo. Like other explorers before her, she became seriously ill in Mourzouk. Upon her recovery, the chief of the Aïr Tuareg offered her an escort of his warriors for the trek over the main part of the desert. At the same time, a party of Hoggar Tuareg persuaded her to accept their protection. This was a fatal mistake. The fame of her wealth had preceded her on all her wanderings. On this, her last voyage, gossip among the natives had it that the metal boxes her camels carried were filled with gold.

Alexandrine Tinne was thirty years old when she entrusted the guidance of her caravan to the Hoggar Tuareg. One day, near a desert well, she tried to pacify some of her men who had started a quarrel. As she raised her right hand in the course of the dispute, one of the Tuareg drew his sword and hacked off her arm; another struck her in the nape of the neck. While she bled to death, they killed her servants and ransacked her belongings.

This outrage touched off a war between the Aïr and the Hoggar Tuareg in which the latter paid dearly for their duplicity.

The man who, more than anyone else in recent times, promoted a sound and peaceful relationship with the natives of the Sahara was General Marie Joseph Laperrine, the intimate friend of Father Charles de Foucauld, although, like Duveyrier, a freethinker. Laperrine organized the camel corps, gathered around him an exceptionally intelligent group of officers and civilians, and contributed enormously to the discovery and comprehension of the desert on his innumerable rounds of reconnaissance. By his kind and understanding nature, his ability, courage and intellectual curiosity, he made friends and inspired confidence wherever he went. As administrator, his conduct toward the natives was one of infinite patience and consideration. In announcing General Laperrine's death to his officers and men, the Commander of the Territory of the Oases said: "Those who have had the honor to serve under him know how great his benevolence was, and what deep concern he showed in obtaining for the humblest what was their due."

During his last moments, lost in the desert, Laperrine had reflected sadly: ". . . and I thought I knew the Sahara!"

In 1920 the first flight across the desert was announced by the French government. An itinerary had been worked out for the five planes that were to participate; relay stations, camel patrols, everything had been prepared on the ground. The goal of this new venture was Timbuctoo. Through a strange combination of circumstances, the commanding general's plane had to turn back shortly after the take-off from Algiers, and the general himself was recalled to Paris on an emergency. Owing to this fluke, Laperrine congratulated himself on the chance of joining the expedition. He caught up with the formation in Biskra. On the take-off for Ouargla, one of the planes cracked up. Before reaching Inefel, another had to return to Ouargla. Nine miles from In-Salah, a third plane had to make a forced landing in a sandstorm. Two of the planes arrived in Tamanrasset.

An enthusiastic reception awaited Laperrine, who was particularly pleased by the presence of an old friend, Moussa ag Amastane, the chief of the Hoggar Tuareg.

The two planes continued toward Tin-Zaouaten, Laperrine's following the slower one of Commander Joseph Vuillemin with the understanding that, if Vuillemin's pilot should go off his course, Laperrine's plane would take the lead. Both pilots were thoroughly familiar with the landmarks below. Nothing could go wrong—except that the visibility dropped to zero. In a haze of dust, Vuillemin's plane went off course.

Laperrine's pilot flew ahead in the direction of the landing point, but in doing so lost his bearings and the other plane. While Vuillemin fumbled along to the Niger, Laperrine's plane ran out of fuel and finally crashed in the dunes. The pilot was unhurt, the mechanic and the general were injured.

The three airmen walked for two days in the direction of a camel trail which they believed to be within forty miles; disappointed, they returned to the wreckage. They rationed their water, biscuits and what little canned meat they had, and sat in the shade of the broken wings. A week later the pilot and the mechanic made a last effort to reach Tin-Zaouaten which, they thought, could not be more than ninety miles away. The general could no longer move with his crushed chest. They prepared two containers of water and cocoa for him and put a tube in each one within easy reach. After dragging themselves over the sand for several hours, they were within sight of the wreck again. They had walked in a circle. Their compass was damaged.

Search parties had gone out immediately and were frantically scouring the desert. Twenty days after the crash, they found the pilot and the mechanic, alive, one hundred and fifty miles from Tin-Zaouaten. Shortly before he died, Laperrine had said to his companions, "I am afraid I have been the cause of your misfortune."

I thought of Laperrine when I said good-by to the French officers at Krenachich. Their love of the desert, their friendliness, their generosity and their good humor made me feel that they, too, were in the grand tradition.

FIVE

HASHRA

1 Sun and Sand

OVER A GLARING WASTELAND OF BLACK ROCK, THE CARAVAN
followed the worn and winding camel trail toward the
south, toward a shimmering lake that was never there. We
were on the stony plateau, the *hashra*, bleak and forbidding
in its immensity and gashed by transverse fissures that term-
inated in a distant range of ruby hills.

Then there was nothing but dead ground and cloudless
sky. The desert no longer offered any points of repair. Eight
hours had passed since morning. I looked at the landscape

critically: nothing had changed. One could hardly call a realm that lacked all growth and all identifying marks a "landscape."

Bani had made a mummy of himself; he was crouching, all muffled up, on his assorted baggage, his knees drawn up under his chin, fast asleep. He was a town Arab, not a born nomad like Salah, who had the courtesy and manners of a grand seigneur.

I asked Salah, "Does anyone ever travel to the east or to the west of the trail along here?"

In his rich, level voice, he said, "No. Never. There is no trail to the east or to the west from here, but it is known that there are great dunes. They are dunes greater than any others, and they are full of very deep holes. If anyone should go there, he would sink into the sand with his camel, and he would never be seen again."

Indeed, to the east and west of us lay regions entirely unexplored, blank spaces on the map, geographical indications being limited to observations along the ancient caravan route.

Najim cautioned me: "If you have to go to the *cabinet*, never go far away, especially in the dark."

The *medjbed*, camel trail, is not one single track, but a passage, often several miles wide, over which each guide follows his particular inclination. On stony ground, the trails are sometimes worn considerably below the surface by the camels; in the sand, the action of the wind leaves no sign of a track. There, only the guide can be relied upon, and he alone decides the direction.

Hashra • *152*

A lead rope came undone; the first camel of the broken file walked off at a tangent, the rest of them shuffled indifferently behind. A *chadam* (camel driver) ran to catch the befuddled beasts and hitched them back to the proper tail.

This was all the excitement for the day.

"Oh . . . oh . . . háha! . . . háha! . . ."

Mile after mile of coarse black gravel over red sand.

We spent a very cold night at the well of Bir Ounane, or rather at a respectful distance from it, because Bir Ounane has been haunted ever since a terrible massacre of Berabish tribesmen gave the place a bad name. No man can sleep in its proximity, I was told, for all night long, while the ground shakes and rumbles, he hears the cries of battle and the moaning of the wounded.

The well was dry, and Najim had no mind to linger as we stood among a litter of human bones: the skeletons of Reguibat raiders who had been left unburied after the battle.

One of the Berabish, Najim told me, saved himself by hiding in the well. He climbed down to the level of the water and remained in the darkness for several days. In a cavity opposite from his hiding place he discovered a large snake. He killed it and kept himself alive by eating portions of it. One night a group of nomads arrived to water their camels. They were sufficiently scared by the evidence of the slaughter that had taken place. When they heard a human voice from the bottom of the well, they fled in terror. But their lives, and the lives of their camels, were at stake. They approached again next morning to investigate the cause of their fright. The voice from the bottom of the well in-

Sun and Sand · *153*

formed them about the preceding events, whereupon they rescued the derelict.

Laazize woke up with an attack of malaria and asked me for quinine before we started out from Bir Ounane. The drivers had not been able to sleep, because of the cold, they said. The butter in Najim's leather gourd was frozen "like that rock, there." The camels had had no water, and very little to eat, for four days. Bani was so tired that he had dropped among his unloaded baggage without eating the night before. Now he hopped along in fits and starts, peering at those around him with his short-sighted eyes, his forearms held curiously upward and away from his body with the palms of his hands spread out as if he were carrying trays of hors d'oeuvres, his loose mouth agape, exposing his awful teeth.

My most valuable possession was an old copy of a Parisian newspaper. It announced that British diplomats had failed to specify England's new commitments on the continent; in regard to the Franco-German conference, it quoted an American source as saying that France must not try to establish economic supremacy in Europe; the spokesman of a French trade journal suggested that Germany import French and Beligian steel since their industries would be the first to benefit by increased German consumption; *Pravda* viewed the whole thing as a stab in the back. The Paris stock exchange was "calmer and more irregular" (which didn't seem to make sense); Egypt was free for the first time since the Ottoman conquest, a lunatic had murdered his family, and at the Porte d'Auteuil an exhibition of chrysanthemums was open to the public.

All this had become somewhat stale and meaningless, but the paper itself served a purpose far beyond the emanation of world news: worn over chest and back, it offered the only efficient insulation against the piercing wind.

By eleven o'clock we were sweltering in the tropical heat, and I then discovered that a *shesh*, or turban, is much more practical than a sun helmet. The wind roaring through the ventilating space around the sweatband of a sun helmet becomes unbearable after a while, whereas a turban can be arranged in an infinite variety of ways to ensure protection against sand, sun and wind. There are cold- and hot-weather turbans. To counteract the midday heat, all of the six yards of material are piled on top of the head; a flowing end may be left behind as a neck guard. If the sun is steadily on the left, the *shesh* can be draped with the emphasis on that side of the head, and vice versa. If the sun is in front, the material can be rolled and stacked low over the forehead. For protection against sand, one loop may be dropped over nose and mouth. Depending on the direction of the wind, a cold-weather turban can be shaped to keep the draft out of the right or left ear, or both; it can be tightly draped across the neck, brought around under the chin, or wound in such a way that the face is completely wrapped up with the exception of a narrow slit for the eyes. This is more than any hat will do, and with a little practice and application a turban soon becomes as easy to wear.

Apart from its utilitarian function, a turban offers a wide scope to the imagination. Some turban-winders stick to an approved traditional scheme and never stray from a conventional pattern. Having formed a habit of tying their *shesh* in a certain way, they would no more change their

Sun and Sand · *155*

system than we would change a fixed routine of parting our hair. But there are those who are fond of innovation, and who will try anything from pyramidal to asymmetrical and absurdly orbicular ones. Turbans can be well proportioned or lopsided, skimpy or voluminous, gay, stately or morose; they may be black or white or any color, suave or loud. The fact is that a turban is the expression of a personality, the mark of a temperament, the key to a man's character. Ranging from the inhibited and severe to the lavish and flamboyant type, carelessly, meticulously or patiently conceived, turbans often are more revealing than faces.

The desert rarely was a flat, even plain, but rather a succession of undulating "swells" with depressions so broad that a caravan seen from a fixed point could be out of sight within fifteen minutes. If and when it reappeared on rising ground, it would be in miniature, far away, proportionate to a centipede crossing a backyard. Being part of the caravan, on the other hand, gave the impression that we were standing still, and that our slow dreamlike drudging was a form of narcosis. Sometimes the rocks thinned out; then we would progress at a good pace over long reaches of hard-packed sand. Once, for several hours, there was no wind. The camels themselves lurched along in a trance. Whenever one of the drivers had to rearrange a load, the animal being handled, disturbed in its abstract reverie and reminded of the stark reality, would bellow as if tortured. To one of the camels a sudden awakening was such a shock that he fell to his knees, screaming. His file had to be stopped but, when pulling would not get him to his feet, Deeah and Houdoud,

Hashra · *156*

the boy, had to separate the beast so that the rest could proceed. They pushed and tried to lift its hindquarters; it only snarled and squealed the louder. Thinking that it might go on if they relieved it of its burden, they took off the salt bars and the *houilla* while the animal whirled its neck to right and left and snapped at them, squirming and bellowing. They pulled and pushed again and kicked it in the groin—all to no avail. Deeah jabbed his dagger in the camel's belly, Houdoud flailed the rear end with his *karouass*; he twisted the tail with all his might, he grabbed the ears and yanked the camel's head about, he bit the muzzle as hard as he could and stuffed the howling mouth full of sand. Nothing would make him rise again.

They hastily drew a circle in the sand around the pack saddle and the salt and placed a few rocks along the line to mark the load as private property to be claimed on a future trip. Then they hurried after the caravan, leaving the animal to its fate.

The ground was rising slightly before us. The abandoned camel crouched in the hollow, a speck of rage and hatred.

It is difficult to find a suitable spot to camp in rocky country, that is, to find a place convenient for couching a large number of camels, for stacking the cargo, and sheltered as much as possible from the wind. Salah was going off his course in search of pasture. We continued traveling into the night and called a halt around ten-thirty in a sandy stretch. Bani sank to the ground with many *"Allah-Allah-Allahs,"* and even the camel drivers were exhausted, but they still had to unload the animals to a symphony of groans and gargles. All night long the camels complained bitterly and cuddled closely one against the other in the cold. They were resting, but they never seemed to sleep. At dawn their hobbles were taken off and within a very short time they had wandered miles away from camp.

Pasture, in the language of the nomads, is one of those vastly comprehensive yet elusive words like soul or love. In these austere regions, where no one comes to stay except to die, in these regions of passage, entered with apprehension and left behind without regret, a pasture is known by a multitude of names—*arraythá, annahem, la'achreef, arrbaia, lo'oukeel*—as if the nomads tried to make up verbally for what the poor soil withholds. The pathetic pasture of the *hashra* consisted of a dry shrub every fifty or a hundred yards. The early morning shadows were much larger than the struggling plants could ever be.

To round up the camels later in the day, the drivers had to run tremendous distances because the animals were scattered far and wide in all directions. If a sandstorm should occur at such a time, there would be no tracks to follow and a caravan would be in a serious predicament. Ordinarily, the men follow the tracks of well-trained camels who will respond to certain calls. The others will then approach closely enough to be driven back to camp. But there are always unobliging ones who complicate the operation and delay the departure. There is a strange poignancy about a lone voice, calling where nothing is in sight, and the sudden appearance of the camels on the edge of the desert.

The route of our caravan was lined with camel carcasses in all stages of decomposition; some were scattered heaps of bones, some parched skins of which the caved-in thorax, eye sockets and shrunken hips had become receptacles for drifting sand. Life followed a trail of death.

"Oh . . . oh . . . háha! . . ."

Many of the animals had bleeding sores on the insides of their upper forelegs, and their mouths were raw where the lead lines pinched the lower jaw.

On rocky ground, walking was difficult; in loose sand, very fatiguing. The hard saddle became an ordeal but, when I was hopeful that walking might be a relief, I sometimes found that my legs were paralyzed, and buckled under me, when I got down. There were moments when I thought the whole thing was badly organized, that the effort it demanded was too much to expect of anyone. The cameleers seemed to be superhuman, their labor out of all proportion to the reward. As for the camels, one could hardly love them; they certainly hated us. Sometimes I hoped that a sudden epidemic would wipe out all camels instantly, but there was no way of calling a taxi. I thought of caviar and Veuve Cliquot and then compromised on a Scotch and soda. The fantasy resolved itself in a drink of brackish water from a goatskin.

Laazize marched forward briskly, perfectly unconcerned about the large holes in the heel ends of his sandals. Bani, with his frowzy beard and a turban three sizes too large for him, bobbed along on his spindly legs, blinking into the sun. He hardly ever spoke, but conveyed meanings by furtive winks and rudimentary gestures. When he was left behind, he hopped after the caravan in a most unnomadic manner and then peered at me knowingly, as if we had a secret in common. I would try to ignore him, but when I stole a glance at him later, his eyes would still be fastened on me while he made jerky little movements with his hands. There was something so demoralizing about this that I would have to rewind my turban to screen my face against him.

In the early part of the day, Najim sometimes talked for hours at a stretch to the camel drivers. Later, when the flies appeared and everyone was drugged by weariness, all energy was funneled into a mechanical determination to continue. The torpor brought on by the sun undermined one's reason. The simplest question could lead into a perplexing coil of absurdity and end in conversation on a dizzy level somewhere between lunacy and the supernatural.

Out of sheer need to say something after looking at the back of my camel's head for several hours, I asked Najim, "Are we going to come to a well today?"

"A well?" he answered, as if I had just invented a new word. "What well?"

"I don't know what well; any well."

"Humm?" (He had developed an exasperating habit of sounding this questioning "Humm?") "A well? What is that?"

"You know damn well what a well is, Najim. *Hassi! Hassi!* Are we going to pass one today?"

"Ah, a well? No. Perhaps today. There are no wells here. Perhaps the day after tomorrow, *inshallah.*"

Implications as oblique as when two blind men say, in parting, "See you later."

The only event within twenty-four hours was the appearance of an almost imperceptible range of dunes to the east: Erg Acheieff. At night we sat down to mushy rice and mint tea with the usual goat flavor and sand.

At the end of a day's journey the camels needed no urging to be couched and unloaded. They were less willing in the morning when everyone was shocked into action by the cold and by the necessity to get under way. The sleeping mats were rolled up quickly, bundles tied, ropes sorted. Bawling camels were kicked to their feet—furious because they were being forced to move faster than was normal for them. "*Arrcup*! . . . get up! . . ." One by one they were led alongside of their load. "*Zaouch*! . . . get down! . . ." If jerking their heads didn't have the desired effect, the drivers grabbed a foreleg, doubled it up, and yanked the screaming brute to his knees. With lightning speed the men moved among a mass of contorted necks and snapping heads. What they could do with rope was nothing short of sleight of hand. They rubbed a handful of cold ashes from the burnt camel droppings of last evening's fire into the worst sores. "*Shidh de rahla*! . . . slap on the pack! . . . Saddle! . . . Sling the bars over the side! . . . Hitch the *guerba* to his flank! . . . Don't forget the teapot . . . *Denni*! . . . off you go! . . ."

They attached the lead lines to each preceeding animal's tail and collected some of the hard secretion of the urine from between the camels' hindlegs. This they crushed and mixed with their tobacco to make the day's supply more palatable. Teeth bared, snarling and gurgling in dismay, the loaded camels moved forward in a lengthening file.

Most of them had brands of bars and dots and circles on

their necks and shoulders, or triangles and flowing Arabic characters on their bellies and rumps; some had their ears split, some had blue tattoo marks on their muzzles which gave them the effect of having four nostrils.

The day was cloudy and the desert drab from here to beyond. The cold wind was biting into our backs and all turbans were wound tightly over nose and mouth. No one was saying a word. The upturned camel pads were blue, the front ones larger than the rear. The loads were creaking mournfully. We had no sooner mounted than the sun came out. It was immediately too hot.

Now—after five hours—we were in a divine *décor* of copper dunes; a marvelous world of pure, abstract form on an enormous scale. The sweeping windward upgrade of each dune was finely fretted by the wind, and from the elegant curve of the *cif*, the "saber's edge," the mass of sand fell away abruptly on the other side in a majestic concave ellipse.

The two passages through Erg Assaderem are the Scylla and Charybdis of the desert. The changing winds either free or sand up these openings. Accordingly, a caravan may have to cross to the east or to the west of the range. At the outset of each trek, the guides try to find out from the last caravan that passed which of the two crossings to attempt.

Salah rode in front, scanning the network of dunes and leading the caravan along a twisting path between the high walls of sand. Bani was picking his nose. From time to time he clapped his hands and wiped them off on his camel.

"Hi-eedi lallah . . . hi-eedi lallah . . ." he sang.

There was something utterly wrong with him but I couldn't put my finger on it.

Hashra · *162*

Five times a day the camel drivers performed their prayers. While the caravan was in motion in the morning and in the afternoon, they usually killed two birds with one stone in that they first knelt to pray and then did their business.

Their day begins at sundown, not at midnight, and the division into hours is hardly known. A minute becomes *ramchi*, the "wink of an eye"; the sequence of twenty-four hours is descriptive, i.e., from midnight to dawn, morning, noon, afternoon, twilight, evening and night.

We reached Foum el Alba, the Gate in the Dune, at sundown; the second important landmark after Krenachich on the road to Timbuctoo. Every caravan has to pass through this breach in the mountains of sand, and every man who comes to this high point in the wilderness must feel that he has arrived at the edge of a lunar shelf.

On the crest of the pass, Salah made a grand gesture *à la* Moses pointing out the land of milk and honey, and ordered the camel drivers to scatter in the endless waste before us. An hour later they came running after the caravan carrying large quantities of camel droppings in their folded robes: fuel for the campfires.

The campfire is the only symbol of home on the camel trail, and a definite social etiquette goes with it. By rotation, one group of cameleers joins another for tea, a ceremony which never varies. First, a shallow hole is scooped out of the sand for the fire and the kettle suspended over it on a tripod. A small metal pot is almost filled with green tea leaves; a hunk of sugar is knocked off a cone with the bottom of the glass and dropped in with the tea. When the kettle boils, the water is poured into the pot which is then moved on to the coals to boil some more. A set of tiny glasses is produced from the *tadara*, a brightly decorated leather bag stretched over a round basket. After ten minutes or so the host takes the boiling tea from the fire and, pouring close to his glass at first, lifts the pot higher and higher with a flourish, causing the tea to rise foaming to the top of the glass. It is then poured back into the pot, and the same procedure is repeated three times without ever spilling a drop. Then the host carefully samples the brew, fills all the glasses, and serves the guests first. The second round is made with yet more sugar, and the third with a dash of dried mint leaves. The first glass is a bracer, the second a pleasure, the third a luxury.

When the water is exceptionally dirty, the camel drivers drop a piece of gypsum in the boiling kettle. This absorbs the impurities. A piece of gypsum is a standard part of their equipment and will keep for several years.

In the hottest weather there is nothing more refreshing than this sweet, fragrant tea. It is also more wholesome than the gallon of ice water which is forever mirrored in one's mind in the Sahara—during the day, that is, for we were sipping our tea on a bitterly cold and windy night, so cold that the hungry camels sighed and groaned continually as they shifted their great hulks to be as close as possible to one another; so windy that we crouched behind the mounds of baggage shivering, unable to enjoy the rice which Laazize had thoughtfully made extra greasy to fortify us against illness.

From time to time I felt that I had been foolhardy, that I had undertaken something beyond my capacities, but of course it was too late to turn back. Any one of a number of things could stop a man from going on with a caravan, things as undramatic as a cold, a blistered foot, severe saddle sores or simple exhaustion, for that matter. There was the possibility of infectious insect bites, of a tornado, of getting kicked by a camel. These were night thoughts, when all the subdued noises around me were signs of weariness and discomfort and the darkness provoked tension and doubt.

On the authority of the camel drivers themselves, the Taoudéni-Timbuctoo trail is one of the toughest in the Sahara. Even today, on a long trek, an aura of apprehension clings to a caravan. The silence alone, spread over thousands and thousands of square miles, becomes oppressive, and it appears dangerous to dwell on the awareness of being in the middle of nowhere for fear of going mad.

In the daylight, self-assurance and a sense of adventure return; the night is dismissed in private embarrassment.

Everyone was coughing until the sun came up. Then Bani recklessly proposed to race Deeah on his camel. The others asked me what I thought of the idea. There was much merriment when I told them that I felt Deeah would surely be *numéro wachad* (first) and that Bani would just as surely break his neck.

The drivers were singing and in a cheerful mood because the rock was thinning out and none of the animals had been injured. The sharp stones frequently cut their pads, and a camel that becomes *mrahass*, footsore, due to such wounds, is useless. Where there are pronounced variations in the nature of the ground over a long route, camels are chosen for certain sections of the trail and used in relays, because some camels are used to sand (as those of the Chaamba), others to rock and gravel; some are more able to bear the heat, others are more resistant to cold.

We had left behind the stony *hashra* and were entering the Azaouad, a region of white sand, the veritable Trab es-Sahra: the Land Where There Is Nothing.

I had not looked in a mirror for a week and now noticed that my nose was severely burnt and puffed up out of all proportion with bloody horizontal cracks. My hands were so swollen that I could barely close them. Three angry ulcers had developed on my knuckles.

All day long we were in the middle of a flat disk of glistening sand. Shoes seemed the sensible thing to wear, but they soon became uncomfortable. What a relief to change to sandals!—except that the sand got into them which made it a torture equal to walking in a bed of hot needles.

"*Zaouch*! Albéwua, old girl. Get down! I can't stand this any longer."

Bani, too, had lost his earlier enthusiasm. He mounted when I did and, from his flea-bitten camel three feet away from me, he said feebly, "*Hyee, labess,* I hope we get to Araouan tomorrow, *Allahi. . . .*"

In the afternoon the sky became overcast and toward evening we were groping along in the eery opalescence of a dry fog (caused by fine particles of sand suspended in the air) which turned into a very black night, blacker than any night before and sinister without the stars. Still, the caravan moved on and on, not straight ahead but in uncertain zigzags, sometimes even at sharp right angles, the heads of the files tense and hesitant tentacles of a vague moving mass wrapped in deep silence. At one point the camel train stopped altogether. Salah studied the wind, carefully examined the sand; slowly we crept forward in the vault of darkness to the mournful night calls of the camel drivers.

"Hoh . . . eeeh . . . hoh . . . eeeh . . ."

Salah and the others had a conference. There was an exchange of opinions in hushed voices and someone held a light close to the ground. We had been guided by the star Zahara, but Zahara was not to be seen and there were no tracks to show us the way. No one said so, but we were lost. The animals had to be fed before morning or they would quit. When I asked Najim how serious the situation was, he only said: "Humm?"

At last we moved along again for another hour, and eventually we descended into a hollow among the dunes, Erg Lemra, where a pile of fodder had been left for the camels.

These forage piles are a matter of life and death, and it is a point of honor among camel men never to disturb bundles of feed belonging to another caravan.

Erg Lemra was notorious because of the many vipers that slithered out of the dunes in the darkness. It had been named after a nomad girl who had died here after being stung by one. All the camel drivers were on guard.

We had traveled from eight o'clock in the morning until eleven o'clock at night without food or rest.

2   *Salt of the Earth*

WHY WOULD ANYONE CHOOSE SUCH A DIFFICULT WAY TO MAKE a living? Why bother to work so hard for something as ordinary as salt?

If salt appears to be a prosaic cargo, it is nonetheless the one item of the caravan trade that has outlasted all others. The slave trade has ended, ivory has given out, gold no longer flows from Wangara, but salt remains an important article in the economy of the native markets of West and Central Africa, and today it is the prime reason for the continuation of so slow and difficult a system of transport as that of the camel caravan. It is so onerous and exhausting an undertaking that the camel men receive three bars out of four for carrying the salt across the desert—a fantastic ratio of compensation.

Only one bar of the normal load of four is the property of the merchant and destined for the open market. The camel drivers may barter their share or speculate with it, as they wish. In terms of money, one bar is worth 150 French West African francs, or 85 cents, at the mines in Taoudéni; upon arrival in Timbuctoo, its value is 750 francs, or $4.25, five times its original cost.* During times of danger and frequent attacks on caravans, the gain was even greater —if the cargo reached its destination, for more than once the *azalaï* was waylaid and became a total loss. In such

* Scale in 1954

cases all the men would be massacred and the camels with their loads were driven off to hideouts and secret pastures by their captors.

From the beginning of man's commercial activity, trading has filled two predominant needs, and the goods exchanged have fallen into two categories: religious and secular. Thus the earliest traffic was in salt, spices and incense.

"Behold, a company of Ishmaelites came from Gilead with their camels bearing spicery and balm and myrrh, going to carry it down to Egypt."

For all its reputation as a country of inexhaustible riches, the Beled es-Sudan, the Land of the Blacks, always has been cursed by lack of salt. Mungo Park, on his first journey to the Niger in 1795, found that "in the interior countries, the greatest of all luxuries is salt; the poorer class of inhabitants are so very rarely indulged with this precious article, that to say a man eats salt with his victuals is the same as saying he is a rich man." Among these inland Negroes a bar of salt was worth twelve dollars at the time. A chip of it given a child to suck was an exceptional treat; it still is, for that matter. In Darfur, a young female slave could be bought for fifteen pounds of salt.

Apart from its ordinary uses in cooking, in the preservation of dried fish and in the manufacture of pottery, the rock salt of Taoudéni is believed to have great medicinal value and is considered as a cure-all for everything from sore eyes to syphilis. Owing to these true or imagied properties, imported commercial salt never has been a serious threat to the magic product of the native African mines.

Salt of the Earth · *169*

An Englishman, Richard Jobson, tells us about a quaint method of barter, the "silent trade," in the early seventeenth century.

'They [the Moors] doe observe one set time and day, to be at a certaine place, whereas houses are appointed for them, wherein they finde no body, nor have sight of any persons. At this place they doe unlade their commodities; and laying their salt in severall heapes, and likewise setting their beades, bracelets, and any other commodities in parcells together, they depart, and remaine away a whole day, in which day comes the people they trade withall, and to each severall layes downe a proportion of gold, as he valewes it, and leaving both the commodity and the gold goes his wayes: the Merchant returning againe, as he accepts of the bargaine, takes away the gold and lets the commodity remaine, or if he finde there is too little left, divides his commodity into another part; for which he will have more, at the unknowne peoples returne, they take to themselves, where they see the gold is gone, and either lay more gold or take away what was laid before, and remaines in suspence: so that at the Merchants third time, his bargaine is finished, for either he findes more gold, or the first taken away, and his commodity left, and this it is saide, they have a just manner of trading and never see one another: to which is added, that the reason why these people will not be seene, is for that they are naturally borne, with their lower lippe of that greatnesse, it turnes againe, and covers the greater part of their bosome, and remaines with that rawnesse on the side that hangs downe, that through occasion of the Sunnes extreame heate, it is still subject to putrifaction, so as they have no meanes to preserve themselves, but by continuall casting salt upon it, and this is the reason, salt is so pretious amongst them: their countrey beeing so farre up in the land, naturally yeeldes none.'

Hashra • *170*

Wherein lies the mystery of this choice product?

The rock salt from the Taoudéni mines does not differ from the commercial variety in chemical composition. Like any other good salt, it is made up of about 96 per cent sodium chloride with another 2 per cent moisture and the remaining 2 per cent minute fractions of magnesium chloride, magnesium sulphate and calcium sulphate. The most searching analysis reveals no mystery whatever, and yet there is one ingredient which does not come to light under scientific examinations: the power of the African mind! The age-old belief in the curative and magic properties of the desert salt makes it an article of trade that defies all competition.

A load of four bars of salt weighs between two hundred and two hundred and fifty pounds. A shipment of twenty thousand bars is quite common. In the years around 1910, sixty-five thousand bars were carried annually from Taoudéni to Timbuctoo; by 1920 the trail had become so unsafe, and the losses through raids so heavy, that the trade fell off to ten thousand.

For the fall of 1954 and the spring of 1955—according to Monsieur Chénal, the administrator in Gao—the number of camels assembled for the *azalaï* was by regions as follows:

Timbuctoo	6,000	
Goundam	500	October
Bourem	2,000	November
Kidal	500	
Timbuctoo	6,000	January
Bourem	2,000	March
Timbuctoo	5,000	April
Goundam	500	

Salt of the Earth · *171*

A total of 22,500 camels.

If each camel, on an average, carried three bars and the bars weighed fifty-five pounds each, this adds up to a staggering amount of salt.

The rate of barter in Timbuctoo is as follows:

16 pounds of rice	= 1 bar
16 pounds of fine millet	= 3
16 pounds of coarse millet	= 2
1 quart of butter	= 1
1 sheep	= 6 to 8
1 camel	= 100 to 110

A certain amount of fluctuation has to be taken into account. Proportionate to the distance from the center of distribution, the rate goes up two- and three-fold.

The *azalaï* sets out for Taoudéni twice a year, the largest camel train usually in November, a smaller caravan in March. Until 1940, caravans of up to 20,000 camels traveled in one group for the sake of security. Now smaller groups risk the trail independently. The northbound caravan (*rebatna*) carries essential provisions to Araouan and Taoudéni as well as black workers for the mines (most of them in debt-bondage) who have to be replaced constantly as the water of Taoudéni ruins the strongest constitution and spells death within a few years.

Oddly enough, this water, so harmful to human beings, has a salutary effect on camels. At the close of the hot season, the nomads of the Sudan and of the Niger colony drive their herds north to the magnesia-charged wells to let them undergo the "salt-cure"—not indiscriminately, but precisely for five days, so that the animals may cleanse themselves in drinking the purgative water and regain their vitality in pasturing on the saline herbs.

3　Nomads

AN EMPTY SKY, AN EMPTY WASTE AND SWISH . . . SWISH . . . swish . . . swish, camel tracks.

Our caravan showed signs of fatigue. Here and there along the files lead cords no longer swung loosely between two animals, as they should, but stretched in taut lines from twisted tails to strained and bleeding jaws. Bani skipped and tottered forward as if he were made partly of flesh, partly of wood, the whole held together by a number of badly functioning mechanical joints. Deeah, our rear guard, complained of pains in his side and lagged behind throughout the morning in the burning sun and chill wind. Then we mounted and rocked again on our camels through the midday hours, a melancholy procession creeping over a hot plate.

A beetle had tried to live here; it left an upturned shell. A tawny lizard passed; there he is: skin and bones.

Najim rode beside me scrubbing his teeth with the frayed end of a stick, a short branch from the *atil* tree which grows in the Niger region and produces these native toothbrushes.

"Najim," I said, "the only thing that is marked on my map

between Foum el Alba and Araouan is El Hajar. Can you tell me what it is?"

"El Hajar? No. There is no El Hajar."

"But it is marked on the map. There must be something."

"No," he persisted. "There is no El Hajar. There is nothing between Foum el Alba and Araouan."

Salah called back to us, pointing to the ground. An addax, one of the largest species of antelope, had crossed our trail a few minutes ahead of us.

These lone animals are very rare. They have retreated to the innermost desert and are hardly ever seen. Their ability to get along on a minimum of moisture is even more phenomenal than that of the camel, as is their instinct for finding sparse patches of vegetation in this universe of sand.

In the late afternoon the camels lifted their heads and stepped forward with sudden zeal. Two hours later a pasture appeared on the horizon. We unloaded and made tea. The liberated animals walked off with a complacent air to graze on the stunted clumps of *hâd*, a spiky gray-green shrub, the favorite food of the camel.

Even Najim revived and became more communicative. I asked him, "What do camel drivers do about women? There certainly aren't any around here."

"Oh," he said, "they have women everywhere. Not in the desert, but in the bush north of Timbuctoo. They always have one or two women in the encampments. Two is better than one because it makes children quicker to work in the camp. Sometimes they have three or four. That is best, but it is more expensive."

Although he could be quite eloquent on occasion, Najim

Hashra • *174*

did not know the terms male and female in French. In referring to camels, he spoke of *chameau monsieur* and *chameau femme,* and children were *petits élèves,* little scholars. Somewhere along the line he had missed out on the word *enfant.* Sheep, *mouton,* had become *la moto* in his vocabulary; when he had eaten enough, he was *trop gonflé,* too blown up.

"Tell me, Najim," I said, "how many wives do you have?"

"I have only one wife," he answered righteously, "in our encampment in the Azaouad. Just one. And then I have only one other wife in Timbuctoo. The one in the Azaouad is white, the one in Timbuctoo is black. They are as different as day and night, and so are the little scholars, three white ones and two black."

"Do they all get together sometimes?"

"No. It is not good for wives to meet. They talk too much, and then they get mad. A man is not the same with different women."

Najim's two wives did not know each other, and he had no intention of furthering their acquaintance. Such arrangements as his are common, though rather secretive, among the regular camel drivers, too, who are away from "home" for months at a time as a matter of course.

There is another, well-founded reason for this: the nomads have a traditional fear of the south because of the many illnesses that are prevalent along the Niger River among men and beasts. Arab women, they say, cannot bear the climate and are subject to premature births and sterility. The Negro women are used to the climate and immune to most of these harmful influences.

Nomads · *175*

The mention of women had made Najim philosophical.

"Everything was decided long ago," he said. "If he wants to live, the little scholar has to accept everything before he is born; his future, his pains, his troubles, everything. If he accepts everything as it is, he will be strong, but if he does not want to go through with it, he does not even come out; he dies right there."

Remarkable people, these nomads: among the poorest and at the same time the proudest of men, true brothers by faith, frugal to the point of asceticism, indifferent to possessions, skillful in finding their way in a world unfit for human life. Believing that man's fate is determined by inevitable decrees, the Moslem has surrendered his will to Allah, for man is nothing, only God is great. Death is so common and so frequent that the thought of it passes through men's minds without undue emotion. "If you will let me live to-day," says an Arab proverb, "you may kill me tomorrow."

Since they have nothing, their generosity is all the more praiseworthy. They will share their last handful of rice with you but, at the same time, they are capable of being hard and cruel in an instant. They will make every effort to help or rescue a man, be he a stranger; in an emergency, even a friend is abandoned without qualms. A caravan cannot be sacrificed for one man; it has to reach a pasture or a well or a point where fodder has been left for the camels within a certain time.

In this harsh land, men exist in defiance of nature, and yet the nomads look down upon the oasis people as Sybarites. There has always been a strong animosity between the tillers of the soil and the Bedouins. Ibn Khaldoun, the celebrated fourteenth century historian, had the greatest respect for the latter. "Sympathy and devotion," he wrote, "that make each individual risk his life for the sake of his friends, disappear when strangled by the habits of a sedentary life." Oasis people know little about the desert at large, a fact which is the basis for a profound contempt among the nomads who, in turn, are despised by the oasis people as worthless vagabonds. To the nomad a house is a breeding place of evil; an oasis dweller would not be found dead in a tent. To the sedentary Arab the community and his possessions are symbols of his security; the nomad takes pride in his freedom from material bondage and enters an oasis only under duress.

Over half the population of the Sahara is nomadic, and although the desert is fiercely hostile to man, few people are so completely in harmony with their environment as its inhabitants. It is almost as if sun, wind, and sand were necessary requisites for a keen enjoyment of life, a faultless hospitality, a courteous manner, a rare courage, and, above all, a wise serenity that has long been lost amidst the nightmares of industrialism. In most cultures, man leaves an indelible mark upon his surroundings; the nomads of the Sahara, born of aridity and silence, are molded by their environment and leave no trace of their existence.

Their endurance and sense of direction are phenomenal. The Egyptian explorer Hassanein Bey reports: "Having taken my bearings, I would control the direction the leader of my caravan was following by my compass ten or fifteen times within an hour. He never deviated a single yard, and it was of great interest to me to watch and to check the perfectly straight course he set across an immense flat region. During the day these desert men have no other compass than their bodies, and their experience is such that they can correct their direction in relation to the sun's movement."

Sometimes the desert is pink and saccharine as a birthday cake, sometimes black and corroded as by disease; bright and alluring as new love or so forbidding that the bravest men shy away from it. There can be no pleasant expectation in a change of scenery; the alternating sandy wastes and stony uplands offer only varying degrees of hopelessness. It is of little wonder that the nomads are haunted by superstitions. The mountains, the dunes, the trees, all are infested with ghosts that are kept at bay with a multitude of protective charms. Before sitting down under a thornbush, the respectful native hurls a stone at it to drive away the *djenoun*. The nomads believe that you must never make a decision when you meet an old or ugly woman, when you see a lone raven in the sky, when two men quarrel near you. Wait for a propitious omen: a good rider, a pretty girl, a pair of ravens. Never, they will caution you, go bareheaded; you will risk sunstroke by day and moonstroke by night. Never sleep directly on the sand; the rapid decrease in temperature after sundown will cause rheumatism and fever. Never drink before eating in the morning or you will be thirsty all day; never drink more than twice a day. Never lose sight of the caravan while hunting; never lag behind. If your skin dries and cracks from sun and wind, don't eat dates; suck an onion and swallow a little goat butter three or four times a day. If a camel has been killed, eat sparingly; an excess of meat will cause dysentery, even death.

Suspended in the middle of infinity, as these desert people are, they have learned to rely as much on their indomitable spirit as on the sparse gifts of the soil. They are awed by the immensity of their world and, along with extremes of stoicism, cruelty and kindness, it has bred in them a singular nobility. They never think of this world as belonging to them; they are travelers on a difficult journey who eventually hope to reach the promised land, a luxurious garden on the banks of the river Tasnim, the paradise of the Koran.

The most famous and revered of all camel men is the Prophet himself. In keeping with the custom of Mecca, Mohammed was left in the care of a Bedouin tribe during his earliest years. At the age of six he became an orphan. When he grew up his uncle, Abou Talib, arranged a job for him to supervise caravans to Syria for Khadija, a wealthy widow. Mohammed discharged his duties so successfully, and his employer was so well satisfied, that they got married, although Khadija was forty years of age and Mohammed only twenty-five. Two sons and four daughters resulted form the union. This was before the divine revelations came to him in the cave of Mount Hirah.

If a stranger were to set out into the desert it would be like plunging into the sea without knowing how to swim, and yet blind men have been known to guide caravans across the Sahara.

When General Henri Gouraud of the French colonial army stopped at the well of Char in Mauritania in 1909, he encountered one Mohammed ould Zoumzoum who, though blind, guided caravans and could point out any direction instantly.

Leo Africanus also speaks of a blind guide, and so does Thomas Pellow, an Englishman who spent twenty-three years in captivity among the Moors during the eighteenth century. Pellow further tells us that "in 1805—so Jackson, who carried on business in Agadir, relates—a caravan proceeding from Timbuctoo to Taffilet was disappointed in not finding water at one of the usual wells, when the whole of the persons belonging to the caravan, two thousand in number, besides eighteen hundred camels, perished of thirst."

4   The Leader and the Led

SIX O'CLOCK IN THE MORNING: THE PERIOD OF GREAT COUGHING.
Our camels had not had nearly enough to eat and were particularly ill-humored and unco-operative: unwilling to get up, unwilling to get down, dead-set against going on.

There were snake tracks all about the camp. How could anything survive in this sterility? The only living creatures to be seen during the day were a few pink locusts with glassy wings who had been blown off their course by the wind and who were bound to succumb to a diet of sand.

My nose was badly swollen and sickly soft; the cracks bled at the slightest touch. Walking in the heavily ridged sand was an awful drudgery, and my mind was dulled by the obsession of unobtainable things as we moved farther and farther into a landscape without any structure, and the caravan floated in slow motion through strata of lighter and darker shades, from pale yellow zones through regions of light fawn toward streaks of cinnabar and distant limpid blues. There was a substance to things in the early morning when the cold made us alert and we were occupied and active before we got under way. Now that we were on the march, and the sun rose above us like a ball of boiling lead, men and beasts looked as if they were cut out of cardboard. During the hottest part of the day all color faded and we proceeded through a fluctuating glare, hardly knowing whether we were going uphill or down because the surface of the desert always seemed to be on a bias, slanting away from us to the left or to the right and suggesting the possibility that a strong gust of wind could make us lose our contact with the ground and send us sliding down the slope and over the rim of the horizon into the bottomless space beyond.

Deeah had crawled on top of a camel before we started and had stayed there ever since, his face contorted with pain. Later he had to dismount. He was quickly left so far behind that he could not catch up with the caravan, weak as he was, barely able to drag himself over the sand inch by inch. Salah stopped the camel train and two of the drivers ran back a mile to pick up Deeah and hoist him on one of the camels in the rear. He was speechless with pain and clung to the hump of the animal for several hours, completely doubled up, until he fell off.

We stopped again. Salah ordered a fire and then rubbed Deeah's side and back vigorously with hot goat butter, but of course that didn't relieve dysentery. Deeah was quite unable to move. The men left a waterskin by his side and our camel train got under way again. Perhaps the caravan that followed ours would find him. Not that they could do any more than we did. If they passed a few miles parallel to our trail, they probably would not suspect anything unusual unless they noticed vultures in the sky. It is easy to find a dead man in the desert.

The east wind was getting stronger and the hot grit raked our hands and faces while the ground blew away from under us.

No one spoke and no one looked back. Each one was concerned with his own survival. Nature offered no encouragement; on the contrary, all the elemental forces were against us, the intruders, and added to our physical exertion a demoralizing sense of fatality.

At first the sand-charged wind whipped over the desert in patterns of fine lace, then, as it gathered force, blinding white ribbons of sand streaked past under our camels. Their tracks vanished before our eyes, the horizon became diffused, the heat was stifling and the sun a pale and evil glow. Only the nearest animals were visible, lurching along in the stinging haze as the caravan cautiously advanced into what seemed like a cocoon, a tarnished silver netherworld.

I asked Najim: "How does Salah find his way here without any landmarks whatsoever?"

He said: "By his head."

All night long the storm kept howling and our eyes and mouths and nostrils were full of sand. We had not had a square meal in over two weeks and the camels were so hungry that some of them were caught eating the fiber saddle packs.

By five in the morning the sky had cleared and we set out toward the Southern Cross. I noticed that my saddle was all wrong when I mounted later in the day; it was much too small, for one thing. Odd, that I had not been aware of it before. It was also pinching in several new places. But in one respect the situation had improved, temporarily: there were no flies. I was worn out after a sleepless night and sat looking past my camel's immensely long eyelashes at the rippled surface of the sand and at the hard shadows we cast on the ground. At times one of the animals would stare intently at a distant point for several minutes, but there never was anything the human eye could see. Huge free-form shapes hung in the sky, and presently we came to a ridge of black rock in the white sand. I inquired of Najim what it was.

"This is Oued El Hajar," he said.

"El Hajar? I thought you said that there was no such thing."

"No. There is no El Hajar."

"But here it is, Najim. Look at it!"

"No, this is Oued El Hajar."

"Well, it amounts to the same thing. You must admit that there is no river, but there certainly is rock."

"No, you said El Hajar. We don't know El Hajar. This is Oued El Hajar."

His contact with the military mind of Europeans had made Najim as stubborn and uncompromising as a commanding officer who has been taught to stick to his position at all cost.

What happened in the past two hours? A load shifted. A teapot fell off.

Now a range of dunes appeared ahead and, from the east, a cloud of yellow dust came racing toward us. The storm was upon us again by the time we reached Erg Djungupaï. Salah rode to the top of a dune to find the easiest passage. He surveyed the land around him and directed the caravan to the right breach with imperious gestures. For a moment it was still and burning hot, then long veils of dust blew off the crests of the dunes around us and within seconds we were in the vortex of a mad whirl of sand that stopped us in our tracks. The ground spiraled up about us, the force of the wind ripped through our clothing and yanked mats and blankets from our packs. Now and then a roaring, as of motors, reverberated among the dunes along with the high-pitched whining of the wind. The camels lay down and stretched their necks on the ground, groaning. The sand piled up against their rear ends; it filled every cranny in the loads, blew down our necks and scorched all exposed parts of our bodies. For several hours we were parched and blinded by the hissing fury of the tempest until we could slowly move ahead again through an opaque mist, dazed and limp after this treatment from a celestial blasting machine.

The sky cleared toward evening, but I had the uncomfortable feeling that we were wandering along the edge of an abyss. We had lost so much time during the day that the caravan continued through part of the night before Salah gave the signal to halt. At sundown the desert had been on fire: like the flash of an explosion, the red flames of the setting sun had swept over the wasteland and up into the heavens where the conflagration was abruptly extinguished by darkness. A prelude to the end of the world? No. Salah, Laazize, Houdoud and all the other camel drivers were perfectly calm and confident, for was it not written that "He covereth the night with day. Lo! herein verily are portents for people who take thought."

A cold wind harassed us as we sought shelter behind the camels and the baggage to eat our gritty rice. It still was a mystery to me how Salah managed to stay on the right course in these difficult circumstances, knowing that scientific expeditions and airmen, equipped with modern instruments, had got lost in bright daylight in the Sahara.

He explained that Zahara, the top star of the Southern Cross, was his guiding mark during the night on the trek to Timbuctoo. "Sometimes," he said, "the star must be directly in the eye, sometimes it is in the left corner of the eye; when we change direction, it may have to be in the right corner of the eye, or perhaps on the left shoulder, or sometimes on the right. . . . *Ah allí therkhél kâhl,* that is the way it is."

"*Allahlahahi . . .*" said Bani, stirring his spittle in the sand.

He could do more unappetizing things than I had ever imagined possible.

It was frightfully cold in the early morning, but the wind had let up. The tip of my nose was badly ulcerated and I hoped that the application of surgical powder would prevent the spread of infection. The white blob in the middle of a sunburnt face looked ridiculous. When I noticed that the camel drivers were excited about something and talked much more than was usual with them, I thought that it had to do with my appearance, but it turned out that they didn't give a damn about my nose. Their astonishment was directed toward something altogether unexpected. They had never seen toilet paper before. Its beauty and its function became the conversation for the day. The world of electric razors and television was absurdly far away from a society in which a match, a needle, a piece of string were possessions to be treasured, and the thought of running water was an extravagant fantasy.

There was very little water left in our goatskins. I was beginning to wonder when we would come to a well. What remained of the water was filthy, and my turban cloth was stained a dark brown from one end to the other from using it to strain the precious stinking liquid from the *guerba* into my own, smaller, waterbag.

A few times on the march I had had frightening palpitations of the heart, a condition I attributed to overtaxing myself. The real cause of it was the strong, boiled tea which, as a steady diet, had an enervating effect on an almost permanently empty stomach. The energy of the camel drivers never ceased to amaze me. How could the human organism, poorly nourished, survive in a climate of such extremes that the very rocks split asunder? How could generation after generation have the hardihood and courage to build their lives on sand? The sand which is so beautiful when you see it as a golden glow, so innocent when you let it run through

Hashra · *186*

your fingers, yet such a deadly menace when it joins forces with the wind. And the wind itself, unpredictable, playfully blowing filigree whisps of dust from the crests of the dunes or whining in sulphurous gusts along the ground, ever present, sometimes gentle as a touch of velvet, sometimes like the lick of a lion's tongue.

Apparently, it is this constant challenge to stay alive where everything is against them which gives true nomads, like Salah, a proud bearing and a noble finesse. Monsieur Chénal had told me about a demonstration of refinement by a man who did not wish to create a sense of indebtedness over a good deed. He, Chénal, was on a tour of inspection in Mauritania. Far in the desert, one evening, he discovered that he had run out of cigarettes. He was astounded when his native guide presented him with a pack the following morning, knowing that he did not smoke. The guide had undertaken a round-trip ride of fifty miles during the night to see a man he knew in the desert thereabouts who, he thought, might have cigarettes. When Chénal thanked the guide for his effort and consideration, the nomad said: "Oh, I didn't do it for your pleasure; I did it only because you are in such bad humor when you cannot smoke."

It is difficult to reconcile such psychological subtlety with an otherwise simple mind.

An enterprising European in a desert post was fortunate enough to get hold of an American bulldozer to dig a trench. This marvelous piece of machinery caused a sensation among the villagers who gazed with admiration as the heavy blade bit into the ground and did work in a few hours which it would have taken them weeks to accomplish by hand. In the course of this performance a nomad rode up on his camel. Calmly, he watched until the bulldozer came to a stop. Then he asked the European: "Do the French make these things?"

"No," said the colonial, "they are made by the Americans."

"The Americans? Hum, if the Americans make these things for you, then the Americans are the slaves of the French?"

"No, no, they make them for themselves as well."

"But if they work for you, they are your slaves."

The colonial had to drop an argument which he knew he could not win, because to a nomad's mentality anyone who does manual labor is an inferior, even if the work is done via the extension of a piece of machinery.

5   *Mirage*

SHIMMERING LAKES LAY AHEAD OF US, COOL AND REFRESHING.

I had learned from the *Encyclopedia Britannica* that such things were due to "progressive variations in the refractive indices of adjacent layers of the atmosphere . . . [and that] a ray of light traversing a homogeneous medium is deviated from its original path by any transparent medium of different refractive index which it enters at an angle less than a right angle . . . [so that] it is therefore readily seen that the path of a ray through continuously varying media is necessarily curved, being compounded of an infinite number of infinitesimally small rectilinear deviations."

Hashra · 188

Fine, but why, when one sees it, is it impossible to photograph a mirage, a veritable mirage, not distorted actual objects? Is it there even when no one is looking? Is it because, trekking along in a stupor of exhaustion, the eye becomes so tired that the mechanism which transfers visual impressions to the mind no longer functions correctly and ends up by producing false images? What seems to be quite near turns out to be several hours' march ahead, so that one learns to judge things generally at a great distance, only to find that, frequently, they are in fact quite near when they appeared so convincingly far away.

"As to the unbeliever," said the Prophet, "their works are like the vapors in the plains, which the thirsty traveler thinketh to be water, until, when he cometh thereto, he findeth it to be nothing."

The Tuareg believe that mirages are created by men who perished of thirst and who are trying to lure the living into the same misfortune.

Anything that moves is bound to be an illusion. The knife edge that was the horizon a moment ago suddenly breaks up into a disturbed jigsaw puzzle. Shapes shift about haphazardly, expanding and contracting, until they are swallowed by a blinding flood. Slowly, elongated balloons rise from the ragged shore, swell to a maximum, each in turn, then, pulled by an unseen force at both ends, they stretch and overlap to right and left and fade away in undulating streaks. Rubber statues come to life, their extremities inflated, awkward in undecisive gestures, bulging at all the wrong points: tottering fever images, monuments shaken by malaria, now rigid for a second, now gradually peeling off to one side, now nothing but lingering fragments of tomfoolery. At times the very ground appears to sway and weave as if all the solidity had gone out of the earth to become a flickering delusion of yawning pits, a wobbly sphere with hazy dents in the periphery. The shrub that seems to be ahead grows to an impressive height, spreads and bedecks itself with foliage, then shrinks to nothing as you approach.

Toward evening, when this phantasmagoria comes to an end, it is like being inside of a monstrous eye about to be darkened by a huge, sluggish lid. During the night the silence is so intense that it has the quality of something yet unnamed: a vast amorphous substance of incalculable weight suspended out of sight somewhere beyond those reassuring stars, hanging by a thread, ready to come crashing down at any moment.

There are no gentle lovers' nights. One is never without the feeling that evil is lurking in the darkness, that the stillness cannot last, that a purpose motivates this awesome silence and this emptiness which have been generating for millions of years. There is a tension of imminent disaster, of a dormant power working up to something as one lies staring at the bland moon, waiting for a shot to ring out, for a cry of agony, for an earthquake to shatter the night.

In the morning the desert about us was black. We had camped on a litter of neolithic pottery. The ground was covered with thick, dark shards, a uniform incised design plainly visible on pieces that had lain face down. There were many jackal tracks about the camp and the coiled forms of serpents lightly buried in the sand. Before we started, another camel had to be abandoned. It had struggled to its feet, but it would not move. It just stood, comatose, with its legs spread wide apart, swaying its head from side to side, scanning the wilderness. The jackals had expected this to happen sooner.

We moved southward over slightly rolling ground.

"Oh . . . oh . . . háha! . . . háha! . . ."

SIX

ARAOUAN

1 The Berabish—A History

THERE HAD BEEN A BLACK SPOT AHEAD OF US FOR TWO HOURS, but we didn't seem to come any closer. It kept disappearing behind the dunes. When we rose to a higher level of ground, it had receded again while it was out of sight. The desert was always playing these little tricks.

Najim's camel had balked when he tried to mount. It could no longer rise on its rheumatic forelegs after getting up on its hind feet. Gurgling helplesly, it had remained in this grotesque position until the load was taken off its back and distributed among the other animals. Then Najim had managed to drag it along. I thought about my conversation with Sidna Ali, and his readiness to replace any of our camels in case they broke down. There was nothing Sidna Ali could do about it, even by remote control.

At last we came to a long, long sandy slope at the foot of an abandoned military post and a few widely scattered houses in a blur of whirling dust. This was Araouan, bleak and wind-swept, a forlorn place in the middle of a vast circle of dunes. Instead of a comforting sensation of having arrived at a safe port, it gave one the impression of having reached the end of the earth. Black children came running to greet us and immediately retreated behind walls, startled and frightened by the unexpected stranger. Some, more courageous than the others, respectfully kissed Bani's hands and then took his camel in charge. They gleefully slapped its rump, pulled its tail and climbed aboard. This, the spooky, ill-tempered beast would not tolerate. It squealed and took several gigantic leaps, lashed out with its hindlegs, and shook itself free from the invaders of its dignified gloom. The boys tumbled off in all directions into the sand and limped along beside us.

These were the first human habitations we had seen since Taoudéni after twelve hard days. The chief's son showed us to a little mud house up the slope while the caravan settled down near the wells in the hollow below. The afternoon heat and the slow, sticky flies brought on a profound listlessness now that the strain of pushing forward was removed momentarily. Najim made a fire to brew tea, fussed with his garments and rubbed hot butter in his beard.

Presently a boy came to announce that we were invited to Bani's house, a quarter of a mile away through ankle-deep sand.

Bani spread a fine carpet: more tea, of course; a large bowl of rice and mutton; sweet, buttered macaroni cut in squares (*leftahd*) and, wonder of wonders, six boiled eggs, something in a shell which the flies had not contaminated. The sand blew in from the offal outside, but Bani was a gracious host to us. The other guests were the old chief, Mahmoud Dahmane, and a young man. The young man told us that his father had never returned with his caravan a few years before. He had left with two other men and twenty-five camels for Timbuctoo. The caravan was caught in a sandstorm. Three of the camels turned up at a well, the skeletons of the two men were found a year later; the young man's father and the rest of the camels were never found.

We had no sooner returned to our house than the chief's number-two wife sent us a live goat as a welcoming present. The Negro butchered it without delay and brought in the carcass to elicit our admiration. Even in the poorest and most remote places the Arab's hospitality never fails. Still, it can happen that a chronic miser will have a servant parade a fat sheep before his guests who lick their chops in anticipation only to discover that the stew, when served, is made of ancient jerky, and that the sheep was merely used as an exhibition piece. In Araouan the custom is to give everything back to the donor except the hindquarters.

Fused with the sand, the glare, the infinite solitude, the low houses of Araouan are hardly distinguishable from the dunes and would escape one's notice altogether if it were not for the black shadows which are the only positive note. All the rest of it seems unreal. But then, the village itself is of secondary importance. Its value as a caravan junction lies in the fifty lukewarm wells. In former days a tax was collected here from all camel trains on their way to Timbuctoo. Father Yakouba, the famous "White Monk of Timbuctoo," wrote in 1921 that "the workers who extract the salt from the Taoudéni mines are the slaves of wealthy Moroccans and of the people of Araouan."

Around 1910 there were about one thousand inhabitants. Although I didn't see more than forty people, the present population amounts to perhaps two hundred. Near the village, buried in the sand, are the ruins of a very ancient city. There is no vegetation of any kind and the people are entirely dependent on the caravans for their provisions. The houses of some of the more affluent citizens have doorways flanked by pilasters which are crowned by inverted earthen pots covered with clay. This gives them a very Byzantine look.

Najim was unhappy because we had run out of sugar. After a protracted search he found a three-pound loaf at the regular current price, five hundred colonial francs, or three dollars.

The old patriarch whom we had met at Bani's house, Mahmoud Dahmane, was the chief of all the Berabish. That night, over dates dipped in melted butter, he told us, in Arabic, about the people of the Azaouad. It was a long, rambling and confused history that began with the year one thousand, "or a little before, at the time of the growth of Timbuctoo, when the Tuareg were in powerful authority and abundance."

Araouan · 198

"The Berabish," Mahmoud told us, "take their name from one Barbush ould Ham Ould Hassan, the Sultan of the Desert. He came with his people to Araouan with many starving camels. The Berabish brought their tents and settled down to make their home in the Azaouad. One of their sheiks was Ali ould Dahmane, my ancestor."

True to form, Mahmoud Dahmane gave us a detailed outline (much too long to mention) of his genealogy, and of the never-ending rivalry between the various tribes. One of the sheiks, he related, had become "so tyrannical and arrogant that he would not permit any other tribe to possess a light-colored mule." There were raids and counterraids.

"Blood," said Mahmoud, "does not sleep."

He then told about the invasion of the Sudan by the Moroccan army under Pasha Djouder in the sixteenth century and the "three thousand archers on camels" commanded by ten generals, with "Farir, the Renegade, on the right, and Wardaoui, the Andalusian, on the left."

After several lengthy quotations from an obscure genealogical work, *The Flower of Information Concerning the Pedigree of the Chosen Prophet,* Mahmoud related that one Muhammad ould Yussuf became sheik of the Berabish toward the middle of the eighteenth century. Yussuf began to extort escort money from those who came to the Azaouad. This led to a scrap with a chieftain by the name of Bid. Bid started the fight; Yussuf later attacked Bid's camp when "the men were at ease, treating their beasts for the scab. They [Yussuf's men] descended among the tents and left them scattered dust. Bid was defeated, his son was killed, and the rest fled. Yussuf died in 1754, killed by deceit after a truce with Bid's people at Araouan."

The Berabish—A History · *199*

There followed a long account of wars with the Tuareg, and with a tribe called Batn al-Jamal (Camel's Belly) "whose light," said Mahmoud, "has not shone since."

I shall not try to fill in the complete and very detailed history which surrounded this story, but jump to the point where the narrator himself was involved.

"I was born in the year [sic] Tjurarat," continued Mahmoud, "which is a place [sic] between Tichit and Oualata where there is a salt mine. In this year the people agreed in council that no *azalaï* should leave with more than ten camels, because salt was very scarce.

"In the year of Amsigil the Berabish rode under the leadership of the amir Sayyid Muhammad. This was my first ride. We reached the territory of the Aoulad Allush, but they fled across the desert. We made a raid on another encampment, killed the men and seized their camels. The Aoulad Allush retaliated and killed seventy-two of our men. We agreed to make arrangements for another raid and were about to mount our camels when we heard that the Christians, the Faranis [French], had encamped at Kabara [near Timbuctoo]. This was in the year 1893. We abandoned the raid as matters had become worse than they were. The black Songhaï people along the Niger River decided to make war against the Faranis, but the Faranis put them to flight. The Christians entered Timbuctoo. They expelled some of the inhabitants and moved into their houses. On the following morning everyone came to look at them and the Christians said: 'We have no need of any people here, either Blacks or Arabs.'

"After that the Tuareg under Muhammad ben Awwab

Araouan • 200

came; a battle took place at Kabara and the Christians put the Tuareg to flight. The Christians began to roam the roads, and no one was able to pass along them without being deprived of his possessions. After this the Christians rode toward the Tuareg, making a raid on them near Goundam. The Tuareg overtook them in a place called Tinbilla and a fierce fight ensued.

"The Berabish returned to the encampment at Timbuctoo and Sayyid Muhammad sent two men to the Faranis that they might obtain a treaty and safe conduct for him and agree to terms. The Christians assented to this proposition provided that Sayyid was present. Sayyid refused to come; so the Berabish set off, resolving to go from the Azaouad to Touat [far to the north]. Sayyid was encamped near Araouan when the Tuareg raided the Azaouad. After this the Tajkanat raided us, and I hurried off in their pursuit in the company of my uncle and my cousin. We caught up with them next day and the enemy was put to flight with the loss of eleven men. I seized one of the men whose name was Al-Bashir, pulling the gun from his hand.

"Then the Christians attacked a tribe of Berabish and left many of their men dead. Next the Adnan and the Tuareg made a treacherous attack upon the Berabish and seized their possessions. The chieftains were in a state of despair and rode to the tent of Sayyid to tell him of their distress. Later I rode off with them and commanded them to do nothing without my orders although there were few men with me. We made a raid on the Adnan and the Berabish were put to flight. However, I remained, surrounded by Adnan who began to pour sword blows upon me, so that not a single one of my limbs remained untouched, but through the decree of God the swords did not mark me. I killed two of their men with my hands, and I wounded many of them, cutting out the eyes of some with my sword and striking off the hands of others. I was young then.

"They continued fighting me and when some of my tribesmen came back, the Adnan retreated. But when we returned to the Berabish in Azaouad, Sayyid said: 'That which has happened is bad, so let the people be on their guard,' and he forbade the people from going on the *azalaï*.

"Later I set out with a small band of men and accompanied them on the *azalaï*, and when we reached Oued al-Aqaw on the way back from Taoudéni, the Tuareg met us at afternoon prayer. When we saw the Tuareg, we unloaded the salt from our camels and we beat our drums. Whereupon the Tuareg thought there was another tribe with us and said: 'We won't do you any harm for we are only seeking the tribe of Ahl ul-Sahil.' I said to them: 'We and the Ahl ul-Sahil are as one, and don't ever attack them during my lifetime.' But the Tuareg arose and raided us, and we fought them until they fled, leaving three dead.

"Then peace occurred between the Aoulad Allush and the Berabish. The tribe of Tarmaz came back to settle in the Azaouad and when they reached Tas ul-Ma on their way back, I forbade them to go further, saying: 'Settle here; I don't want you to be in a place together with us.' This was because they had acted treacherously at first and our souls rejected them.

"Then came the year in which the Christians withheld food from the people of the desert. The reason for this was that Sayyid had sent a message to them in an unsuitable manner. When the Christians withheld food from the people, Sayyid sent a message to the chiefs of the Tuareg, asking them to assist him against the evil wrought by the Christians. It is a fact that the people who had suffered at the hands of the Christians on previous occasions had never made any agreement except that now requested by Sayyid. I rode to Timbuctoo and when I saw the harm done in the land through the people's lack of food, the evidence it offered of the Christians' strength, and that war would only engender war, I acted swiftly in what was best for the poor. I arrived in Timbuctoo by night, met the chief men, and they came to an agreement regarding the Christians. They told the Christians that I had arrived. In the morning, when the *muezzin* called from the tower of the mosque and the day arose with success, I went to see the Kamandakal [commander]. He asked me my business. I replied: 'I have come to request you to cease withholding food from the people.' He said: 'We only withheld the food because of the message Sayyid sent us.' I said: 'You helped him, and if you withhold food, the land will fall into his hands.' On hearing this, the Kamandakal was pleased at depriving the people of food. This was the first disagreement between my cousin and myself, for Sayyid claimed that I disagreed with him over the command of the tribe.

"Meanwhile, Sayyid had sent a message to the Tuareg to gather together for a war against the Christians. When they came to him, he apologized for having summoned them, and he let them down by not going to war with them, saying: 'Mahmoud has aroused the mass of the people against me.' Thereupon they went to the river and began to loot the possessions of the Blacks. The troops of the Christians came upon them and they fought together. In that year we raided a tribe of Kel Antassar [Tuareg]; then they raided the Adnan. The brother of Anagunn made peace with the Christians. The following year Anagunn rode until he alighted near the Kel Antassar; here his brother came to him and Anagunn rebuked him for having made peace with the Christians without his permission.

"The Christians heard of this, approached him unawares, and surrounded him. He looked left and right, but found no way of escape. The troops told him to go along with them to Timbuctoo. When he had gone with them for an hour, he fled from them to a stronghold of his, but his son Muhammad remained in the hands of the troops until they reached Timbuctoo. Anagunn came in search of his son, and whilst climbing a high hill, he was shot by one of the troops, dying on the spot. As for his son, they let him go with a safe conduct.

"In this year there came a new Kamandakal who rode until he stopped at Ankum, which is the name of a well. Here he met one of the chiefs of the Kel Antassar and made a peace treaty with them. Then he returned to Timbuctoo and sent a message to Sayyid requesting him to meet him at Mount Tadarara, but Sayyid refused and rode off in the direction of Araouan after the Kamandakal had sent him a message, saying: 'If you didn't like us gathering near your tent, we shall come to Araouan.' Sayyid was at Bou Djebeha; he ordered me to go to Araouan to prevent the Christians from entering it. I refrained from this, sending a message to At-Tin who was in Araouan at that time, and At-Tin prevented the Christians from entering. Urwa, the chief of the village, went out to them alone. The Kamandakal said to him: 'Let us give water to our camels. We have only come to do good to the land, not to wage war.' So he let them do what they had requested, and they returned to Timbuctoo.

"In this year Ibn Humaid killed one of his wife's people, Ben Abbas, unjustly, and the murderer fled. The sons of Abbas demanded justice from Sayyid, but he refused. So they came to me. I requested Sayyid to grant them what was due to them and that if he didn't do so, I said I would leave him. I departed and encamped at Tagant Keyna [Little Forest]. At that time the Christians came to Warzil and burnt all the food there when Sayyid had fled into the desert. Then he sent a message to me demanding that I come to him, but I refused. We went to the well of Tanta-houn and there encamped with certain tribes of the Berabish who sought rest in my presence. God, however, willed that Ibn Humaid, the killer of Ben Abbas, who was previously under the protection of Sayyid, should return in search of some of his camels which had gone astray. I said to the brothers of the murdered man: 'The murderer is near, so go and kill him.'

"When they had returned from killing this man, I went to Timbuctoo where I renewed our treaty with the Christians. Then I made a pact with Sayyid to join the whole tribe. One day sixty-six Reguibat halted at the tent of Sayyid as he had sent a message asking them to come. They agreed to waylay me. I had some of Ben Abbas' men with me, but they fled leaving me to fight on my own. God helped me against my opponents and He put them to flight although there were thirty-one of them. Then I told the Reguibat: 'Go back to your lands and, by God, don't ever let me see you again!'

"The following year the Tuareg of Hoggar and Iforas rode out in large numbers and raided the area between Arsh ul-Akhal and Tamghanana, seizing three hundred she-camels and killing many men. When they got back to their people, they sent a message asking to make peace and to cease hostilities. We accepted their request on condition that they give us two camels yearly.

"Then the Christians asked for a thousand camels, so that they might raid the land of Hoggar. The Berabish refused, and the Christians imprisoned many from every tribe so that the Berabish fled into the desert. I rode after them and collected five hundred camels. The Kounta rode off and attacked the Tuareg as the Christians had been helping them with supplies. Then the Tuareg made peace with the Christians.

"The following year there occurred a split between Sayyid and myself. The Christians asked me to come to them, and the Kamandakal ordered me to bring those of the tribe who were with me, so that he might imprison them. I refused, saying: 'Leave us alone until we know who of us will be the victor and who the vanquished.' The Kamandakal refused, and I said to him: 'If you must imprison my people, take me instead of them,' and the Kamandakal did so. Later I returned to Bou Djebeha and went with the *azalaï* to Taoudéni where Colonel Lagsib [Laperrine] had arrived. He was the first of the Faranis to go there.

"Now the Aoulad ul-Ahjour raided the Azaouad many times and attacked the *azalaï*. The Berabish fought them until they fled. Many of them died of thirst and some came to Timbuctoo to seek peace.

"Then the disease known as *ḳawan* killed many of our camels. At this time raids were too numerous to mention.

"In the year Khazatat [1921] the Reguibat raided Araouan and captured part of the *azalaï*. I was in Timbuctoo, and the Colonel said to me: 'Rise and go swiftly until you catch up with these people.' I instantly rode out at the head of a party of my men and we did not sleep day or night. We followed the enemy to Lamghit, seizing them, their guns and camels. Their leader was called Anoush. When the Reguibat raided again, the Christians proceeded to Anhoun and took six hundred prisoners. They were then brought to Timbuctoo where many of them died.

"In the year 1928 Captain Maril, known amongst the Arabs as Bou Dabbous, the Man with the Club, came and governed.

"In 1930 the Reguibat put themselves under the protection of the Faranis. Then the year in which our sheik At-Tijani died; may God bestow the amplitude of His mercy upon him.

"Then the year in which the people disputed with Muhammad Mahmoud in the month of Mawlud [the festival of the Prophet's birth] during which disputes are unheard of, for those happen only in the month of Ramadan.

"In the following years there occurred nothing of note."

The Berabish—A History · *207*

It was during those years—so uneventful for Mahmoud Dahmane—that Hitler exterminated over two million Jews, that great cities became masses of rubble, and Japan experienced an atomic blast.

All this had made no impression whatever in the Azaouad. To a Berabish tribesman nothing could be more disastrous than a raiding party of Reguibat.

2 A Touch of Fever

NEXT MORNING THE CHILDREN STILL SCURRIED, SHRIEKING, behind the nearest wall when I stepped out of our house into the blinding sun and the raging wind. Some of the inhabitants gathered in our enclosed yard to have tea with Najim and Laazize, others boldly entered the house and sat down on the sand floor to get acquainted with me. Our visitors were extremely polite, but when one is in a weakened condition to begin with, it is peculiarly unnerving to be subjected to ceaseless observation, to be stared at and considered as a weird curiosity. It is particularly disconcerting to be laughed at for having clean habits, although I certainly couldn't brag about going to extremes. In fact, I was developing a nasty skin rash, possibly because there had been no opportunity to take a bath for well over a month. I was covered with ugly little red spots and itched from head to foot. Of course, our diet had been rather one-sided, too.

The young son of the village chief, who had half of his

head shaved and wore the other half of his hair long, brought a friend of his, an emaciated boy with a ghastly cough. The poor fellow had a burning fever and obviously needed more than a couple of aspirins. To compensate for my medical limitations, I gave each of them a pencil, a pen-knife and a cheap notebook. The sick boy was starry-eyed and overcome with gratitude.

"Now, every time I open this book," he said, "I shall think of my friend who came to Araouan."

Araouan is strictly a watering station for caravans, not an oasis. There were no oases this far south; only shadeless waterholes. The dark seas of waving date palms belonged to the northern deserts of Algeria and Morocco.

Like everything else in the desert, the construction of a well requires a tremendous effort, and so does the watering of the camels. At the head of each well are two wooden forks which support a horizontal pole with a pulley in the middle. In most cases the wood has to be brought from hundreds of miles away. A goatskin attached to a metal ring serves as a bucket (*dellou*) which is hauled up time after time by a camel walking away from the well at the other end of a long rope. A Negro, the *hackam dellou*, takes care of the tedious job of emptying the bucket into a trough or a suspended cowhide, giving a yelp every time the goatskin comes to the surface as a signal for the boy leading the camel to turn about. The moment the operation begins, the waiting pack animals converge upon the well, awkwardly heaving their large bodies forward on three legs, one of the forelegs usually being bent and tied up at the knee to keep them from straying. Camels habituated to long treks always drink their fill, conscious, apparently, of the long intervals between watering points; inexperienced animals without this superior sense of proportion, or those ordinarily used for shorter marches, lack this foresight and often fail to drink enough. They are the first to weaken on the trail.

Najim's camel could go no farther. He made a complicated deal to exchange it for Bani's disagreeable but enduring beast. The situation was a golden opportunity for a squeeze and I fully expected to be sucked into a costly financial operation, but nothing of the sort happened. They were scrupulously honest.

Was I exceptionally lucky? Or did a natural affinity with these Moors make them accept me without reserve? The testimonials of early travelers are consistent in their condemnation of the desert peoples' cruelty, their cunning, rudeness and intolerance—traits easily associated with their recent activity as slave drivers, marauders, cutthroats. Could people with such an infamous past and such a vile reputation become good fellows overnight? Or were they, the Berabish included, unjustly maligned in the first place? They always considered themselves quite virtuous in comparison with their traditional enemies, the Tuareg.

We were all a bit the worse for wear despite our short rest. For the camel drivers it wasn't a rest, really, what with watering the animals and checking and repairing the pack-saddles and the loads. Najim's wooden box, our symbol of opulence, had gradually disintegrated to such a point that it had to be held together by ropes. Most of the nails had worked themselves out and the lock had got lost somewhere in the sands of the Sahara.

Now the caravan was under way again; a long, dark thread twisting over the deeply corrugated pattern of the dunes along the proverbial trail of bleached bones. Just as we had not seemed to be coming any closer in approaching Araouan, it now appeared as if we could not get away from it. The town itself was lost immediately among the vaporous furrows, but the sharp square of the abandoned fort remained in sight for over an hour on the high ridge. The quality of the light, the nature of the scene, the disproportion of things, made this world a doubtful reality in which no one could move freely without grave danger. All, except those of superior knowledge, had to be led, and sometimes even a guide strayed into the Land of No Return which was full of bottomless pits. The trail we followed was like a tightrope suspended in space, without a net beneath us.

"Allah it is who hath raised the heavens without visible pillars; and then ascended his throne, and compelled the sun and the moon to perform their services."

What was left of the goat's hindquarters bounced on the flank of our pack animal in the process of being cured by flies. As the heat filled the air and the wind burnt our faces, the midday drowsiness left me in a half-doze until the camel stumbled under me and made my spine shoot through the top of my head. The accumulated fatigue was general; the men no longer walked off a way into the desert to perform their prayers, but smoothed the ground before them where they happened to stop. Kneeling in the direction

A Touch of Fever · *211*

of Mecca, they rubbed face, hands and arms with sand; bowed, stood up, scratched and kneeled again; three times in earnest communion:

La illaha illa Allah
Mohammed razul allahi . . .

Laazize usually prostrated himself and went through his genuflections immediately after the evening fire had been started, mumbling ecstatically to himself and kicking the dust into the stew pot.

By the following day the long sandy ridges alternated with depressions of black volcanic residue, again and again and again. In contrast to the carefree Tuareg journey, there was no singing and no music on this trail of hardship. The camels had become much weaker in their protests and followed one behind the other like so many wound-up automatons, each one of their sores a little worse than the day before.

The surgical powder had worked wonders on my nose; there was only a general soreness now, but the skin rash was making me itch all over.

There was no use in asking: "How late are we going to continue tonight?" No one knew, not even Salah. To ask him would have been nearly as out of place as to address a personal request to Allah. The thing to do was to steel oneself for another three hours in the last extremity of weariness. Several times I managed to get myself into a trance which eliminated all consciousness of time and discomfort. The trouble with this system was that then, without warning, the caravan would stop, the signal would be given to couch the animals and, before I had time to function in the present, my camel would collapse under me when I least expected it and I would barely escape from breaking my neck at the end of a perfect day.

And then I realized that it was Christmas, and nature presented a wonderful gift: a morning without wind. I probably suffered from a sensational vitamin deficiency by now which had to be corrected with fresh fruit and vegetables. That evening I celebrated by taking my one and only can of stringbeans out of the wooden box. I read every promising word on the label and pried the lid off with my jackknife, having lost the can opener, too. I don't know how many years the can had reposed on the shelf of a tropical native store in Gao. Or perhaps stringbeans and camels don't mix? Anyway, instead of the revitalizing garden greens that I expected, a malodorous foaming mold bubbled up. The poker-faced Moors, who were watching me, had won another round. The practical food in the Sahara is rice and sand.

The landscape had become an endless vista of hillocks with tufts of ragged weeds. The sand was too soft for walking, and riding the stumbling animals meant perpetual jolts. We had come so much farther south that the nights were no longer as cold as before, but the sun was fierce during the day and the insects had increased in numbers and variety. The ropes between the camels' tails and jaws were nearly all stretched out full length; even the wildest ones were docile now, too tired to put up a fight when they were being loaded. Salah still strode along in the loose sand as if

A Touch of Fever · 213

he were just starting out, oblivious of the raging wind. Najim crouched on his camel holding the guiding rope between his toes. His face was uniformly dark; the white of his eyeballs never showed, so that the only noticeable contrast were his teeth when he opened his mouth, which made him look rather fiendish, especially at this moment when my head was swimming from fatigue and everything was a little blurred. I couldn't remember when or where we stopped, but I had the sensation that I was falling, deeper and deeper down, for a very long time, with Najim grinning high up above me. When I finally regained my footing, I found that I was walking on suction cups—or so I imagined, because it really was deep sand that held me back, a steep slope of sand which kept crumbling away under me. I had to get to the top, I thought, even if it was the last thing I did, and the effort was worth it, for when I reached the crest of the dune, I saw tents spread before me and gay streamers drifting in the wind. There were music and laughter in the air, and at the foot of the tablelands in the far distance a city of blue domes and arches rose from the ashen rock. The tents were open except for a thin netting, and the only voices I heard were those of women, beautiful and more than friendly, judging by the ones I saw. One, in particular, caught my fancy: a slim, seductive girl with olive skin, exquisitely delicate and sensitive, whose name, Ghazal, I knew without asking. Had no hunter spied her? It seemed odd to find her unattended. She was dressed in the most persuasive scent, and her dark eyes said: "Come to me."

I entered her tent and all fatigue and anxiety vanished as

desire surged within me and all my senses filled with rapture at the fervor of her passion and the touch of her accomplished caresses. All my being yielded to this revelation of delight. I had never known such amorous perfection, such sweet and sensuous abandon, such artful flights to the very brink of consummation, and, after moments of voluptuous restraint, fulfillment so joyous and harmonious. There was an interlude of languorous tenderness while I held her breasts with the painted nipples and lovingly retraced the intricate triangular design which graced her beauty. She smiled behind her long lashes, when a gruff voice commanded me to rise.

Outside the tent, black men were waiting for me with a string of camels.

"*Ach tehabb?*" I asked the one who had spoken. "What do you want?"

He sneered, and said: "We come to promise you a grievous punishment."

Their camels had fancy trappings and the men carried spears. I knew that I could not argue with them, so I mounted the animal which was pointed out to me before the caravan moved off in the direction of the distant city. Slowly, silently, we rode over the scorched earth. Once we descended into a deep cleft which had not been visible in looking over the dazzling plain from the tents. It was deadly still between the walls of rock, and the heat lay like a heavy carpet at the bottom. As we emerged from the canyon on the other side, the wind ripped into us again. Half-empty goatskins, horrible, perspiring carcasses suspended from the saddle, wobbled at my knees, and I was very tired. It vaguely

A Touch of Fever · 215

occurred to me that I would lodge a formal complaint with the authorities of the region when and if I got out of this jam, but I had no idea what region we were in.

Our destination was a huge square, teeming with glistening blacks and other natives in gaudy attire. They all jeered, and it was very discouraging to think that there was no way of reaching them with a kind word. They were effulgently hostile. I was trapped.

At the far end of the square, under a canopy, sat the Caid and, by his side, to my amazement, I recognized my friend, the British colonel, who was chained to a post and fuming with indignation. He gave me a shaky "cheerio" and said to the Caid: "I say, old boy, aren't you rather doing us down?"

Somehow, the court interpreter must have conveyed the gist of the remark in Arabic, for the Caid replied: "We only laugh at weakness."

I was shaking uncontrollably, partly from fear, partly because of the sudden chill in the air as the sun plunged behind the mountains. The flickering light of the torches, which now illuminated the square, and the crash of wild drumming, added to the sinister atmosphere.

Then there was silence, the ominous silence of the desert, and the voice of the Caid, the black libertine, saying: "Speak unto the believing women, that they restrain their eyes, and preserve their modesty, and discover not their ornaments, except what necessarily appeareth thereof; and let them throw their veils over their bosoms, and not show their ornaments, unless to their husbands, or their fathers, or their sons, or their captives, or unto such men as have no need of women, or unto children, who distinguish not the nakedness of women."

The multitude assented with a pious murmur.

Then the drumming resumed, pandemonium broke lose, black hands were raised against me. There were shouts of "Dweller of the Fire! . . . Cut off his head! . . . Cut off his head! . . ."

"*Hamdullah*," said the Caid, as a slave grabbed my arms and another started to swing his scimitar.

The last thing I heard was the voice of the colonel.

"Ruthless, these chaps . . ."

A red flood engulfed me. . . . I was shaken by a prodigious spasm. . . .

3   *Cram-cram*

IT TOOK ME ALL OF NEXT DAY TO GET OVER IT.

A sunstroke, perhaps? Or a touch of fever? I was still shaking, and utterly worn out. Najim was by my side.

"*Tu veux bouffer le riz, un peu?*" "You want a little rice, maybe?"

He had made up my bed in the lee of one of the hillocks and brought me a glass of tea which greatly revived my spirits. Laazize sat a little way off among the slabs of salt, looking uneasy. I could see the camels browsing through the tall weeds; how slow, disdainful, unconcerned they were! Near me, a large black beetle scampered off into the wide, wide wilderness with admirable determination. It was early morning.

I took an extra dose of Arelin and ate a few spoonfuls of the greasy rice.

"Thank you very much, Najim."

By the time the caravan started up again, I had pulled myself together sufficiently to stagger south beside the melancholy camels. My ears were ringing and I was shivering from intermittent chills. The day dragged on in glare, in heat, and in interminable hours. There was no sign of life when we came to the well of Tagant Keyna, other than the bugs that crawled over us all through the night. The forest consisted of a few stunted thorn trees, a welcome sight nevertheless, and the first indication that we were about to enter a new territory, the *asharrg*, the region of the bush. This, also, was the northern limit of the belt of *cram-cram* (Cenchrus biflorus), a terrible, scrawny weed, two feet high, with thick clusters of sharp, tiny burs which attach themselves to anything that brushes against them, enter the skin, and can truly drive a man out of his mind. It is undoubtedly one of the nastiest plants on this earth, and yet, in times of famine, it has often been a lifesaver to the nomads, for each armor of needles protects edible grains which can be cooked as a cereal.

The camels took no notice of the change of scenery, although the *medjbed* now was a broad, churned-up trail, the same that had been used for many hundreds of years, the route of the intrepid eunuch Pasha Djouder who was sent in 1590 by the Sultan of Morocco, El Mansour d'ed Dehebi, the Victorious and the Golden, to take possesssion of the

Taoudéni salt mines and to crush the Songhaï empire in the far Sudan. With eight thousand camels and over three thousand fighting men, recruited among Moors and a rabble of Christian renegades, Djouder's spectacular caravan crossed the Sahara in one hundred and thirty days. It was he, and the descendants of his Moslem musketeers, the Roumas, who spread the faith of Islam among the pagan tribes of the middle Niger. The fabulous loot of gold, slaves and ivory, with which he returned to Morocco after his bloody conquest, gave credence in Europe to the legend of Timbuctoo.

Riding was more uncomfortable than ever before: the camels kept swishing their tails and shifting their hind-quarters, and every few minutes they violently shook their heads when the flies crept up their nostrils.

Najim, who was walking, suddenly became alert. In scanning the ground, he had singled out a human footprint among the countless camel tracks.

"I know this man," he said after a while. "He is a captive from Rarous." He was as pleased at seeing the man's marks in the sand as if he had met an old acquaintance.

Most nomads have an uncanny gift for identifying tracks. By studying the imprints of a party of men and camels, they can deduce their exact number. They can tell whether the animals were loaded or not, and whether they were fresh or tired. The condition of the droppings may indicate how long ago a caravan passed, and where it last stopped to pasture. In the eyes of the nomads, the lines on a camel's pad have the individual characteristics of human fingerprints. They hardly ever fail to find an animal they know when they go after it, no matter how confusing the crisscross of other tracks may be. In claiming a stolen camel as their property, they can give so detailed and concise a description of its four pads that their incontestable familiarity with the animal will discourage the most obstinate thief.

The zebras, and the lion tracks, which the explorer Oskar Lenz saw on his journey in 1880 south of Araouan, had disappeared, but there still were gazelles about, and that evening Najim took his gun out of the dust cover, spent fifteen minutes rubbing and blowing, and went hunting.

He must have walked a considerable distance before he saw any game, because it was well over an hour before we heard him fire three shots, far from our camp. Another hour passed until he returned, empty-handed, covered with *cram-cram*, the gun braced across his neck.

Luck had been against him. He told us that he had wounded a gazelle, but that he had not been able to follow its blood spoor long enough because of the darkness. So our menu remained unchanged. We didn't tell him that a well-fed buck had walked leisurely past the camp within fifty yards of us during his absence.

Salah settled down on a mat to dig the stickers out of Najim's legs with the point of his dagger. Our animals lay couched nearby, looking over our heads with cynical expressions and contemptuous sneers. I asked Salah if he could offer any explanation for the camel's conceit?

"*Aiwa,*" he said, "there is a good reason for everything, for 'Allah knoweth, ye know not.' This is how it came about: Every true believer knows that there are ninety-nine names in praise of Allah, the Merciful, the Beneficent, the Mighty, the Bountiful, the Clement, the Forgiving, the Cleaver of the Daybreak, the King of the Day of Judgment, the Lord of the Worlds. . . .

"These every true believer knows, but what every good Moslem also knows is that, in truth, there are a round hundred. And this, the highest praise of all, no one has ever known.

"The Prophet said: 'The camels have we appointed for you as symbols of your obedience unto God, ye also receive other advantages from them. Wherefore, commemorate the name of Allah over them when they are standing on their feet disposed in right order, and when they are fallen down dead, eat of them; and give to eat thereof, both unto him who is content with what is given him, without asking, and unto him who asketh. Thus have we given you dominion over them, that ye might return thanks.'

"Now, when the Prophet was about to enter the gardens of eternal abode, clothed in green garments of fine silk, he called his favorite camel to his side, and he whispered something in his ear. And the camel, aware of being the only creature to hold the secret of the hundredth praise of Allah, has felt himself superior to man ever since."

There was just the faintest breath of daylight over the horizon when Najim and I set out after the wounded gazelle. He picked up the trail without difficulty where he had abandoned it the previous evening. A quarter of a mile farther on we discovered the place where the animal had lain down. It had bled profusely but, still, it had dragged itself along. The track of a hyena now ran parallel to that of the gazelle, and presently we came to a thorn tree under which the hunted animal had died. Here the hyena had gorged itself and left a new trail where it had slunk off after the feast. The most recent track was that of a jackal, who had followed the hyena. He had scraped the ground all about under the tree and had scattered the bloody bones. Ants swarmed over the remains, and vultures slowly circled overhead. There was nothing left for us.

This was the kingdom of the ants. The whole country had been taken over by them and the soil elaborately tunneled over thousands of square miles with underground thoroughfares terminating here and there at the metropolis of a certain clan. They all resented intrusion, for the minute one sat down to rest, ants of every description converged in silent attack. There were bold, large, clumsy ones; a quick, active, medium-sized type; microscopic febrile ones; some lacquer-black, some a dull red, others that seemed to be albinos: all of them bent on torture, and some so ill-tempered that they devoured each other.

Later that day there was a curious, low-hanging cloud ahead of us which was no longer in evidence when we approached where it should have been, until a great whir filled the air around us. The thorn trees exploded. We found ourselves smothered by a dense swarm of locusts, a cloud of flashing wings. The hard bodies crashed into our faces and against the slabs of salt. Masses of them were maimed and squashed underfoot, but the remaining legions would strip the trees of every leaf.

Still, destructive as they are, even locusts serve a good end. They can be the salvation of a starving caravan, when the camel men collect the dormant insects in the early morning and crush them into a paste. Dried, this will keep indefinitely and can always be reused, mixed with water. There are more ways than one to survive in the desert with a little ingenuity—and luck. As a last resource, a recipe which originated in the Tibesti region might come in handy: select a bleached camel bone, pound it into a powder, bleed your camel, stir the blood and crushed bone until smooth, add salt to taste.

This is preferable to boiling one's sandals (also a recognized emergency dish) because it avoids the trouble of making a fire and does not deprive a man of indispensable equipment.

On the whole, it was wonderful to be surrounded by greenery; wonderful to be among trees again, even thorny ones. With this thought I gratefully prepared my bed for the night, flicking away a twig from the outer cover of my sleeping bag. But the twig, ten inches long, did not brush off, and when I picked it up, the little branch came to life in my hand, not vigorously, but with a slow, drugged motion; just sufficiently to cause surprise. On closer examination, I found that it had legs, three additional little branches, at the tips of which were clinging feet, and at one end of the main branch of this angular contraption, straw-colored and cataleptic, was the semblance of a head.

Some sort of a giant walking stick? My companions didn't know. They grinned and shrugged their shoulders indifferently.

The camels, so sharply defined in the region of sand, where they seemed to belong, now appeared as strange

Cram-cram · *223*

antediluvian creatures half-hidden among the trees. They craned their necks at the top branches, straining after the tender leaves, or stood in bizarre attitudes of fixation, their hindlegs crossed awkwardly, their lips drooping.

In the bush the caravan traveled in three separate files, each section following the most convenient trail among the thorn trees. The calls of the camel drivers echoed back and forth.

"Oh . . . oh . . . háha . . . háha . . ."

And now another menace made itself felt: ticks. There were millions of them, in the trees and busily hurrying along the ground; they crawled on our arms and legs and down our necks until one's whole body shrank in revulsion from these hordes of steel-shelled little bastards. Stepping on them in anger did not have the slightest effect; they went right on their way, impervious to the formidable blow. Ground into the sand, they re-emerged with undiminished vigor. Their little wire legs found passages through our hair and under our belts. To me it was particularly disagreeable to have hundreds of ticks superimposed, as it were, on a skin already aflame with a rash. Give me the clean bite of an ant any day.

Salah picked up a thorn and calmly spiked some of the ticks that circulated within easy reach. This was the only time I saw him laugh.

I gave up the fight as they tickled and nipped me while I tried to sleep, thinking, without conviction: "I'll catch you in the morning."

That night, after all the walking we had done, the quiet

Houdoud took a hike to visit a girl in an encampment; on foot, a round trip of five hours.

During the next day's march our surroundings changed again, this time to a vast steppe of *mrokba,* low brush, very coarse and drab, which camels will eat only *in extremis.* This was still the desert, but the vegetation, though far from lush, gave it a decidedly Sudanese flavor. It did not have the grandeur of the empty wastes of sand that we had left behind; instead of being awe-inspiring like the silent country of the dunes, this was a sad, dust-green immensity depressing beyond words.

We stopped for some of the camels at the well of Boyot, a bleak and deserted circle of trampled ground. Not quite deserted; two ragged figures rose in the distance and came toward us. They told us that they were headed for Araouan. They had heard about me. One of the men complained of stomach pains, so Salah got out his medicine bag and boiled a dried herb, *agaia,* which is also used externally for wounds or injured camels. Before long they were engrossed in their one inexhaustible subject of conversation: the Reguibat. As usual, reference to time was absent in their stories, and one couldn't tell whether the events alluded to had occurred the day before or twenty years ago.

There never is one nomad; there are always two, and they are always looking for company to gather around the teapot for chitchat.

Toward evening we were on the trail again, flea-bitten, dust-covered, the camels plopping drearily through the clumps of low brush.

After weeks of an exceedingly monotonous fare, my

mouth fairly watered when we found ourselves right in the middle of a herd of large, white Dama gazelles. Some of them stood looking at us almost within reach, others trotted lightly from shrub to shrub. One of them would have been enough for a feast, but the men kept on talking and Najim took so long to disentangle his gun that they all faded away without once breaking into a run.

There was a slight disturbance at the head of our file; we had to make a detour around an enormously blown-up and putrid carcass of a camel that lay with its neck stretched on the ground and two legs grotesquely up in the air. The underside of the body had been torn open by an early connoisseur.

We also passed an artificial mound, for which Najim gave the following explanation: One day a band of forty Tuareg came to a Berabish encampment here and made an offer to trade camels. The Berabish stalled, and told the Tuareg that they would deal with them the next day; in the meantime, they told their visitors, they were welcome to stay in their encampment. Apparently, the Tuareg had no evil intentions. They were perfectly confident and peacefully retired for the night. But the Berabish were afraid of them. Although they had no quarrel with these particular Tuareg, they did not trust them on principle, and so, in order to avoid unpleasantness, they waited until dawn and, at a given signal, massacred all forty of them.

I couldn't very well ask a Berabish what happened when the rest of the Tuareg found out about this piece of treachery. The story of their revenge would have to be gleaned from the Tuareg.

Araouan • *226*

We camped in a clearing in the brush that had just been vacated by a hyena. The striped, crouching animal trundled off barely fifty yards, then turned and lay down to watch the unexpected activity in its domain. The camel men paid no attention to it; what one can't eat is not worth hunting.

All through the next day the landscape was the same dismal wasteland of dry, spiky shrubs. Usually, the early hours were still, but by nine o'clock the wind came hissing out of the east and tall pillars of dust reached into the white sky.

It is difficult to comprehend why human beings fought so long, so bitterly, for the control of such an inhospitable region, yet it was officially insecure until 1936 when the Reguibat were finally subdued.

Our first test of endurance, each morning, was the ordeal of marching into the glare of the sun; during the rest of the day, the caravan crept up and down the never-ending undulations of the ground under a cupola of tropical heat. The camels, tired as they were, tortured beyond endurance by the innumerable flies, tossed their heads and suddenly rushed forward to rub their faces frantically against the preceding animal's tail to relieve themselves for an instant from the black pests that stung their nostrils and sucked the oozing puss in their eyes. They were peppered from head to foot with *cram-cram*, it was impossible to touch them anywhere without getting those deadly burs all over oneself.

Najim's behavior had become very mysterious again. We were all so hungry, and there was so much game, that it was most exasperating to watch him hunt with so little enthusiasm. He rode at the head of the caravan, but he kept talking and shouting to Laazize even when a herd of gazelles was in view. Had he quietly walked ahead a few hundred yards, alone, he could not have missed. Instead, in some strange way, he always gave gazelles and antelopes full warning. After the game had fled, he stubbornly set out in pursuit, ignoring such fundamental rules as stalking against the wind. Of course, he knew all about these things. He was a trained fighter, after all. If I had not been thoroughly aware of a cruel streak in him, I might have thought that he had some moral compunction about killing a gazelle. Time and again he had every chance to score a clean hit, but, every time, he muffed it, as if he felt he had to put on a show but preferred to save his ammunition.

More than once I felt like yelling at him: "*Hchalá mourád Allah*, man, give me that gun!" But I didn't want to make him mad at this late date. I never understood the deviousness of Najim's mind.

4   *The Last Lap*

DURING THE LAST LAP OF OUR JOURNEY A NUMBER OF OUR camels were so fatigued that the caravan had to deviate a few hours' march from the trail to find replacements for them in a pasture. Such arrangements are made sometimes in the open desert in the absence of the owner, who may not hear about the peremptory loan of his beasts until he can be found, months later. In the meantime, the animals which are left in exchange represent a legitimate security—provided they don't succumb to the aftereffects of exhaustion.

The vegetation had become quite impressive and the desert was more like a parkland by now. There were mimosa trees and flat-topped acacias and broad-leaved fleshy euphorbias. The only element that spoiled this idyl was the inescapable, closely-knit tangle of burs. As we entered the wide hollow of a dry river bed, a flock of six ostriches crossed our path. They were running at high speed in single file, scooping a trail of deep holes out of the sand.

While the roundup of fresh camels was in progress, Najim put up a welcome shelter for me against the scorching sun, and one of the men brought us a large bowl of fresh camel milk. Toward evening we got under way again, wading through solid *cram-cram*. In the darkness, Salah found the direction back to the main trail by the silhouettes of trees that were familiar to him.

"The stars are blue," he observed. "It will not be cold tonight."

His prediction was perfectly correct.

The following day we crossed the caravan trail to Goundam, the only intersection on the entire trip. Long-horned zebu cattle wandered through the bush to left and right and, though we didn't see a soul, I was told that there were many nomad camps in the vicinity. In the afternoon we arrived at Agonigefal, the Hole the Camel Fears: two wells at the foot of a tremendous, solitary dune with the plain of thorn trees sweeping away into the wavering heat. Three Negroes greeted us with much politeness; around the fringe of a

The Last Lap · 229

barren circle of manure a few donkeys lay panting, twitching their ears.

We passed the rest of the day in a torpor, muffled up
against sun and flies, and that night we went to sleep to the
sound of lowing cattle and barking jackals, faintly aware,
toward dawn, of the swishing tread of a caravan and the
muted calls of cameleers. We left the dune of Agonigefal at
an early hour, and later in the day caught up with the section of the caravan ahead of us and with the camel train
which had passed us during the night, both of them being
camped along the trail.

Two captives with a few animals stopped on their way
north. They seemed depressed. One of them had lost a sandal
on the trip down from Araouan a month ago. He wanted to
know if we had seen it. Talk about a needle in a haystack!

Tomorrow, I thought, we would enter Timbuctoo in
triumph, but Najim cautioned me that we would not arrive
in daylight. This, he said, would be too dangerous as many
of the camels were half-wild and would be frightened by
anything unusual. He told me that, a year ago, a caravan did
enter the city during the day, but that the animals became
so panicky at the sight of all the people that they bucked
off their loads and charged out of town into the bush.
Some of them were being picked up still, he said, as far
away as Morocco.

There was no hurry now; we were within a day's trek
of our destination. We had plenty of wood for fires, and
the fear of getting lost or running out of water lay far behind us in the Azaouad. All along the line, among the
gurgling beasts, the camel men gathered together in little

groups to talk about their latest experiences or the vague legends of the past while they fortified themselves with sweet mint tea. Despite their unimaginably hard way of life, they were cheerful and wonderfully dignified and, though they spoke the harsh desert dialect, their voices were agreeable and subdued, and there never was the slightest hint of vulgarity.

In the afternoon, we commenced to load in a leisurely way until two parallel lines of camels stretched way ahead out of sight and slowly started to amble southward. Among our newly acquired animals were a number of females with spindly-legged young who soon got bored walking obediently beside their mothers. Occasionally, they crossed over to the other file, nibbled at thorn trees, or lagged behind. At this their mothers, tied as they were, grumbled softly and craned their necks to keep an eye on the wayward little ones.

Black and white birds with extravagant bushy tails flitted about under the tamarisk; gazelles bounded through the *cram-cram*; an eagle swooped down out of the blue for a closer look at the caravan.

And then the *azalaï* became a string of shadows in the night as the long, long files moved very slowly through the darkness to the rhythmic clacking of the salt bars and the high-pitched whine of chirping insects. Laazize was lost in cabalistic mumblings by my side and some of the men were fast asleep on their camels—a dangerous thing to do, particularly in the stony desert where a fall on a rock can easily result in broken bones. One of our cameleers was rudely awakened when a branch very nearly knocked him off his perch.

There was a pungent odor of decay and wildlife in this stifling corridor among the trees and, now and then, breathtaking whiffs of concentrated creosote issued from our ill-fed beasts as they broke wind. A bright half-moon rose over the fringe of the bush which was alive with wild night cries, mournful hooting and hoarse chuckling sounds in its depths.

Again, as in the gloomy stillness of the desert, I had a premonition of disaster—just nerves, of course, and exhaustion, I told myself, although I could not get rid of a feeling of tension which seemed to have alerted the drivers as well. As if by an unspoken command, they had all swung down on their camels' necks to the ground and, from the head of the caravan to the far rear, the men kept the animals lumbering along with their soothing calls.

"Aaah . . . eeeeh . . ."

"Aaah . . . eeeeh . . ."

Cautiously, the shadows moved forward into the darkness, ever so slowly, as if danger lay ahead indeed. The little ones had long stopped capering about; they now stayed close by their mothers' sides.

Ten o'clock . . . eleven . . . midnight . . . hour after hour, the same unnerving monotony, the forced wakefulness on the brink of sleep, the stupefying chorus of the insects. . . .

And then it happened. There was a crash among the dead branches . . . a wild beast started up in the bush . . . in an instant the middle section of the caravan was utter chaos. Camels screamed as they yanked themselves free and plunged into the night, shedding their loads . . . salt bars cracked with the sound of gunshots . . . pots rolled on the ground . . . drivers sprang to catch the flying ropes. . . . Part of one file got tangled up in a thicket while the men tried desperately to keep the rest of the camel train under control. Animals stood, shaking, petrified with fright . . . some collapsed on the spot . . . some strained at their jaw-holds and blindly bumped into one another, stamping their feet. . . . Only the droning of the insects remained unchanged as huge birds winged away from their hideouts in the trees, and the darkness was filled with choking dust.

The men had to tramp through the woods for an hour to coax the terrified fugitives back. Then they gathered up the debris, got things in order as well as they could, and calmly set the camel train on its proper course again. Yard by yard, we crept forward, until it seemed that our journey would never end.

At last, at two o'clock in the morning, we descended a slope of deep sand toward a darker streak in the darkness: the bell-shaped huts of Abaradyou, the caravan terminal of Timbuctoo. There was no reception committee, no fanfare; in fact, there was absolutely no one about. We had merely transferred ourselves from one vacuum into another. Timbuctoo was a dead city, without a single light.

In hushed voices, the men discussed the most delicate part of the operation: the entrance into the city of the various sections to deposit the salt in different quarters. Many of the camels had never seen a house or heard a dog bark, so that the greatest care had to be taken to avoid further mishaps. They were rather a pitiful sight, these listless beasts, with their bleeding lips and their shoulder flesh gouged out inches deep, but their expressions seemed to say: "We only sneer at weakness."

I bid Salah and the others good night as they walked off with their assigned loads. I had looked forward to some sort of a celebration at the conclusion of our trip and was perfectly willing to contribute my share, but this was no time to make social arrangements. After such a long and hazardous undertaking, it was something of an anticlimax to disperse so unceremoniously.

Najim, Laazize and I struggled through the loose sand with our four camels down a broad lane between mud huts and little courtyards screened off by palmetto mats, across an immense empty lot, past a row of square clay houses, and finally into a walled enclosure around a tumble-down adobe building with a wide veranda on one side and plenty of bats.

Najim asked Laazize to fetch the cook, the last person, I thought, we needed at this time of night. Then we couched the camels and stacked our things against the wall.

The cook, when he appeared—a sleepy, none-too-happy Negro carrying a candle—had no intention of preparing a meal, and I was far too weary to think of food. He led me to a room furnished with a rickety table, a broken-down chair and an iron bedstead complete with torn-up mattress. While I took in my new surroundings, he chased a rat half-heartedly, placed the candle on the floor and vanished without a word.

"We have arrived," said Najim, flashing his teeth.

SEVEN

TIMBUCTOO

1 Today

NEXT MORNING NAJIM LED OUR CAMELS AWAY, PROMISING TO be back later.

The mud-streaked walls of my room were a fine facsimile of the Niger delta in which the dirty stains suggested swamps and cockroaches represented crocodiles. The top of my mosquito net was full of rat tracks. The window shutters were festooned with spider webs.

The surly cook—the only native on the premises who had a smattering of French—had to be handled with kid gloves to give any service. Since the door of my room could not be shut, there was a constant unannounced coming and going of the various black members of the household; and even total strangers walked in to shift the wobbly chair, to spit on the floor, or merely to take a slow look around. This procession was sufficiently creepy, but the ultimate criterion of courage was the stinking latrine: a symbol of indifference to the weary traveler, and to life and death in general.

One of my visitors was an *évolué*—an educationally advanced Negro. He drifted in as I was having my coffee.

"You want woman?" he asked cheerfully. "Nize girl, anytime; black or white,* as you wish."

Prostitution for breakfast; I declined, and I didn't feel that I owed the fellow a lengthy explanation. But my calculation was wrong, for no sooner had I stepped into the back alley on my way to the authorities to present my credentials, than a chorus of black wenches greeted me with shouts of *"Bonjoo, Moosieur N'aime-pas-la-femme!* . . . *Bonjoo, Moosieur N'aime-pas-la-femme!* . . ." This was so patently unfair that I tried to correct the misunderstanding. After all, I had just arrived with a caravan and deserved a rest, even though an eighteenth-century chronicler claimed that "a stranger who enters Timbuctoo cannot do without women. The food and the climate provoke concupiscence and put men in condition to perform prodigious feats."

The resthouse in which I was staying, the only lodging available to a white stranger in Timbuctoo, was an old clay structure badly damaged by successive rains. The main ap-

* *White* meaning Arab

proach to it was through a rubbish heap in the administrative part of town with the infirmary to the left, the Palace
of Justice opposite, and the cemetery to the right, all at a
considerable distance across a stretch of whirling dust.

A broad avenue of sand led past the post office and barracks to a vague square with the residence of the commander, the police station and other administrative
buildings grouped around it. Beyond this were the dust-
colored two-story houses and the narrow twisting streets of
the fabled city.

The French officials received me with refreshing cordiality.

"So, you are the *caravanier américain!*" said the officer to
whom I presented my passport. "We have seen all kinds of
people, but this is a new wrinkle. We have seen journalists
come through here like meteors. They took one look and
. . . *pouff*, they were gone again. You have really come the
long way! Friend of Monsieur Chénal, eh? Fine administrator, one of the best. Of course, Gao is much more of a place
than this. Please sit down. I imagine you have been on your
feet long enough."

He stamped my passport with great care.

"This doesn't happen very often, you know. I want to
give you a clear impression. You'll want your friends to be
able to read it. There are not many passports with a Timbuctoo stamp in them. A fellow in a jeep got stuck a hundred miles from here not long ago. He couldn't quite make
it. The best he could do was to have his picture taken in
front of a signpost that said Timbuctoo."

The official was so friendly that my visit seemed like

Today • *239*

something that might happen in a dream world rather than in a police station, and yet he was by no means exceptional, for a most generous and hospitable attitude was extended to me from all sides.

I next stopped at the little post office to ask for my mail. The African clerk brought a whole stack of General Delivery letters from another room and cheerfully dumped them all in front of me with the request to sort them myself. Most of them, I noticed, had been there for several years, addressed to travelers who, evidently, never had reached Timbuctoo.

Then I had my first look at the town.

To be in Timbuctoo gives one the distinct satisfaction of having arrived in a place that has become a byword for remoteness, and which has been the scene of one of the most intriguing phases of African history; to actually see it is quite a shock.

Whole sections of it are nothing but ruins, and in every quarter there are houses washed out by tornadoes or collapsed from neglect with grass huts and palmetto shelters in the vacant spaces here and there. It is a ghost town, a very remarkable one, not only because of its lurid past, but because the present inhabitants themselves are a living testimonial to another age. For one thing, none of them seem to work for a living. They stroll about in magnificent *boubous* (a sort of toga) as if they were in the Garden of Eden. The outward signs of an African gentleman in Timbuctoo are a flashlight, which is carried even by day, and an umbrella (against the sun). The children run about the streets stark naked.

It is a "backward" city; there are no neon signs, no taxicabs, no post cards; there is no industry, no advertising, no movie theater, not even a hotel. A new white man is a sensation.

As I struggled through the sand into the center of town, the Arabs stared, the Negroes chattered, the Tuareg fastened their penetrating eyes on the stranger from the outside world and solemnly raised their right hand in greeting; the women in the market place clapped their hands and broke into song. All of them, except the Tuareg, wanted to have their picture taken. This was surprising enough, but it was even more extraordinary to be asked if it would cost them anything! They didn't expect to get a photograph; they merely liked to pose—stiff as ramrods.

The black women who crouched under the torn raffia mats suspended over low supports in the center of the market obviously didn't expect to become powerful merchants. They sat amidst the buzzing flies with a few greasy honey cakes or a wet rag full of kola nuts mainly as an excuse for enjoying the animation around them. Under some of the tilted mats were bowls of rice and millet, under others gourds of liquid goat butter, dried fish, spices, wood and charcoal, sandals and other leather goods, cheap imported kitchenware and plastic trash. There also were a few trays of semiprecious stones, relatively high in price (each worth several dollars) because they had been blessed in Mecca, and a necklace or two of the richest gold. Or was it? No. They were examples of filigree work in henna-stained straw over small shapes of wild bees' wax, an ancient art of the Songhaï Negroes that is just about lost.

The stalls along the inner wall around the market were

occupied by butchers, bakers and merchants in hides, cotton goods and cutlery. All these things were being carefully examined by local Songhaï and Arab customers, and by the Bozos, Dogons, Bambara, Mandingoes, Kountas, fuzzy-haired desert Berbers and Fula herdsmen who happened to be in town. Among the women shoppers, those of the upper classes could be distinguished from the servants by their built-up hairdos, such as tightly dressed upstanding disks interwoven with strings of cowrie shells, which set them apart as ladies who never carried anything on their heads.

The commercial activity in the market was on a small scale. There was business in a big way, too, but all important transactions were conducted behind closed doors, a tradition dating back to the years when the Tuareg were a constant menace to the tradesmen.

In the streets adjacent to the market were small native stores and two French trading posts. Everywhere, along these streets, men squatted in the sparse shade quietly conversing, letting the world go by. When anyone entered one of the little shops, a number of loafers immediately congregated at the threshold to watch the proceeding and to offer advice to the purchaser. Water carriers trotted past to households in all parts of the town with dripping goatskins on their heads, and Tuareg warriors with straight swords at their hips swaggered about as if they owned the place. Bush people stood on one leg, leaning on their spears, the other foot braced against the inner thigh. Coy black women issued from wooden doors studded with iron ornaments. A leper passed, his chest scarred by frightful open sores, his face a mass of bloated deformity swarming with flies.

One thing I needed urgently was soap.

I passed through the crowd of loitering Africans into the general store and marveled at the wealth of canned and packaged goods displayed on the long shelves, the rows of tinware and kerosene lamps, the stacks of sugar cones and sun helmets, the bolts of brightly colored fabrics and sacks of rice and tea.

The black clerks waited on their exotic customers at a pace so slow that it made one think they all were afflicted with sleeping sickness. The Frenchman who managed this operation was in startling contrast to the general coma. He appeared from an inner office and introduced himself briskly: "Bobet, agent of the CFAO [*Compagnie Française de l'Afrique Occidentale*], at your service."

I asked him about soap.

"Soap? Certainly, all you want—" and to one of the clerks —"Soap! Toilet soap for Monsieur, and quicker than that!"

Then he turned to me again. "In case you are interested, we also have Cravenna. Shipment just arrived. Hard to believe, but it did arrive. We don't get Cravenna every day, you know . . . just in case you are interested. . . ."

For a minute I didn't know what he was talking about. Cravenna? He handed me a can. I was very glad to have it: Craven-A, English cigarettes.

There was a bagful of gnarled brown peas beside me on the counter. I asked him what they were.

"Parasites," he said. "Typical of the country. They grow on roots in the Niger marshes. We call them *tara*. They smell nice. Here, all you have to do is scratch them a little. The ladies like to wear them in their bosoms."

Today · 243

The clerk had returned, and I now had a demonstration of what the tropics can do to people. On the whole, it made them lethargic but, all of a sudden, it provoked great spurts of energy, usually in the form of a first-class fit. Monsieur Bobet was a thoroughly nice fellow, but many years in the West African climate, with bouts of anemia, dysentery and malaria, had brought him to the edge of hysteria. This was no condition in which to deal with employees who were either under the influence of a strong sedative or part of the great African conspiracy to drive the white man, if not out of the country, then at least out of his mind.

"I said soap!" yelled Monsieur Bobet. "Soap! Not flea powder! The gentleman didn't ask for flea powder! He asked for soap! Do you know what soap is? Flea powder is what you need, you black impenetrable idiot! But I want soap! . . . Soap! . . . SOAP! . . . Do you understand? . . . No, you don't understand . . . you don't want to understand! You want to be a savage! . . . Well, as far as I am concerned, you can put back your nose plug and eat grasshoppers . . . but before you do, give me that soap! . . . S-O-A-P, you understand? . . . Not grasshoppers! . . ."

The clerk stood there, dull, expressionless, unimpressed. Then he went sleepwalking back to the dusty shelf.

"Sorry," said Monsieur Bobet to me. "Come on back and have a drink. I tell you, a fellow can be here twenty years and he still won't know what makes these people tick."

What made this Frenchman tick was his basic kindness. I saw him again the next day, and many times after that. The clerk was still there, and Bobet was like a father to him.

He had a wonderful hunting dog, a very elegant, sleek, long-nosed *sloughi*. These *sloughis* can match the speed of a gazelle and are trained to run alongside of their quarry, knock it over and bite its throat.

"Yes," said Bobet when I admired the animal, "he is a fine dog. He does everything he is supposed to do. He runs alongside of a gazelle, he knocks it over, he runs back to it as fast as he can—and then he stands there, licking it, to apologize for what he's done!"

I had lost twenty-five pounds on the trek with the caravan. The food at the resthouse was such that it seemed as if the cook had made a special effort to render it unappetizing and unpalatable: nondescript soup, heaps of oily bones, or pulpy, lukewarm fish were the order of the day. Aguibou, a very primitive boy from the hills of Bandiagara, was greatly distressed because I would not eat the hideous fish heads. His knowledge of French did not extend very far beyond *Oui, Monsieur* and *ça va*. When I asked for a plate, he brought a cup, and when I wanted a fork, he brought a knife. He served the sugar in a cylindrical tin that bore the label and contained the remnants of a medical powder for skin disease. In the heat of the day, even indoors, Aguibou wore a heavy old khaki army overcoat; at night he stripped to a pair of shorts and donned a battered sun helmet. I asked him: "How do you like Timbuctoo?"

"*Toumbouctou,*" he said, "*ça va—un peu. Bandiagara, c'est mieux.*"

Africans are deeply attached to their home ground. Aguibou had got sidetracked in the capacity of boy to an expedition and was waiting for a chance to return to his wild hills where his kinsmen had flourished until very recently on cannibal fare.

What saved me were the wholesome meals which the kind American missionary asked me to share with his family from time to time, and the generous invitations from the commander, the doctor, the officers and Bobet, the genial trader. There were perhaps thirty-five Europeans in town, all told.

I saw no signs of oppressive colonialism in Timbuctoo. The administrators I met showed a genuine interest in the country and its people, and their attitude was one of understanding, tolerance and patience in dealing with exasperating situations—mostly cases of theft or involved problems about a wife or a cow, and sometimes thorny political issues. On the lighter side, there was the case of the rogue hippopotamus.

All along the middle Niger, the people keep horses who pasture half-submerged in the marshes. A little way down the river from Timbuctoo, a number of these horses had come to what truly might be called a sticky end. A lone hippopotamus had taken an intense dislike to them. During the day, when he floated in the water, he could hardly stand the sight of them. At night, he would waddle up on the banks, pick out a victim, and squash it in the mud. He had disposed of sixteen horses in this manner. The river people had never been able to catch up with him, although sometimes he came ashore close to their villages where their canoes were beached. He had trampled some of those into the ground, too.

The administration agreed that it was time to take a firm stand. A campaign was mapped out, and the delinquent hippopotamus was brought to heel.

There were devoted scholars among the civil and military officials, men who spoke several native languages and who were working on research projects on their own initiative. They were pleased to "belong" where they were, and to understand their complex surroundings, despite the demoralizing effects of the climate. The few exceptions were precisely those who did not belong. Some of these modestly hinted that they had been indispensable links in the resistance movement during the war, and that they had performed daring deeds to liberate their country.

"But look at it!" they said. "We finally got rid of the Germans. Now the Jews and the foreigners are ruining France!"

One of the local dignitaries I met by accident as I was walking down the street. A superb figure of a man decked out in a jet-black beard and crimson robe approached and, in excellent French, asked me—as if I had broken a previous appointment: "I thought you were coming to see me. I am Mohamed Mahmoud."

I had heard of him, indeed, and told him that I had looked forward to meeting him. Monsieur Chénal had spoken to me about him—in rather guarded terms.

"You *must* come to see me," said Mahmoud with a friendly petulance which could not be ignored. "I am the Cadi [judge] of Timbuctoo!"

Opinions about this personage, and even about the gentleman's official standing, were divided. His political affiliations and his business operations were believed to be somewhat questionable from the French point of view. I had no way of judging this and found him a keenly intelligent and courteous host.

Aguibou had shown me to his house in one of the innumerable, nameless, twisting streets in the center of the labyrinth of Sankoré, the residential section around the famous mosque. Like other native houses this, too, reminded me of a tomb. A dark staircase with perilous, worn-out steps varying in height from five inches to two feet, led to the upper floor. There were no tables; there was very little furniture of any kind. The standard equipment for living were large earthenware water jars, a painted wooden chest or two, a few gourds, wooden bowls and palmetto mats to sleep on. (Only the Tuareg use spoons; the Arabs and the Negroes eat with their fingers.) The interior of Mahmoud's house was unusual in that there were two wicker chairs—exclusively for European guests—among the orthodox furnishings of rugs and leather cushions.

He showed me with great pride a library which consisted of a bare room full of huge piles of books and priceless manuscripts in Arabic—including a copy of the Tarikh es-Sudan—all under a thick coating of dust.

Mohamed Mahmoud was in no way related to Mahmoud Dahmane, the Berabish chieftain. In fact, I sensed that there was no love lost between them. The Cadi's main object was to inscribe my name, my nationality, and the reasons for my visit in *his* chronicle while we drank mint tea. Perhaps he added a few remarks after I had left. Actually, he did most of the talking. He did not ask me a single indiscreet question. It surprised me that, though an Arab, his historical views were tinged by a pronounced respect for the Tuareg, particularly the branch of the Machsharan (the Strong) who, according to him, were in charge of the region from the decline of Moroccan rule to the time of the French conquest. The representative of these Tuareg, he informed me, bore the title of Koyra Koy (Master of the City, in Songhaï), and Mahmoud himself had assumed this title which, apparently, was honored by the citizens.

The great majority of the citizens are Negroes. Timbuctoo is a black city. It lies five miles north of the village of Kabara, the "port" which is connected by a channel through the marshes with the Niger River. When the water level is high, one of the lagoons swells to the limits of Baghindé (the Refuge of the Hippopotamus), the northwest quarter of the city. The bush trail, now a road, from Kabara to Timbuctoo, always has been one of the most notorious haunts of bandits and cutthroats in all the Sahara and the Sudan; the scene of countless robberies and murders. The loneliest stretch, the favorite point of ambush, is known as Our Oumaira: No One Hears (the cries of the victims). In conjunction with the French administration, the city and the region are under the supervision of a Songhaï chieftain and an Arab cadi. Songhaï and Arabic are the predominant languages next to Tamachec (Tuareg) and Koroboro, a local dialect. The quarters of Sara Keyna and Sankoré, to the east and northeast respectively, are the native residential section, fringed by the beehive huts of Bellah captives. The livestock market and the *medersa,* the Arab college, are on the western edge of town along the lagoon.

At one time there were many more trees, but the Moroccans cut them all down when they needed timber for boats to patrol the Niger.

The small airstrip near Kabara is sanded up; the nearest landing field is at Goundam, seventy-five miles to the southwest. From there the mail is brought to Timbuctoo by military trucks. A power plant produces electricity for a few hours at night, but it doesn't always work. With the darkness the bats come fluttering low over terraces and courtyards, and lizards wiggle into the lamplight to feast on the profusion of insects. Most any night a crowd of Bambara or Songhaï will come together near the lagoon or in the southern end of town to sing and dance to a rippling xylophone and a spine-chilling drum that hums, roars, thunders in complex patterns and imperceptibly increases in tempo until it vibrates and throbs at incredible speed without ever misisng a beat. In the old days this used to go on all night; now the law forbids drumming after 10 P.M. because it is offensive to European ears.

In the outlying quarter of Abaradyou—which is inhabited by all manner of spirits, vampires, fetishists and sorcerers—a brisk nocturnal trade is carried on in charms and *grigri,* the most common type being little bits of paper on which are written Koranic invocations or magic formulas. These are carried about specified parts of the body in small leather satchels. Apparently, there are masters who deal in much stronger medicine as well to judge by widespread whispering about dark practices.

One evening I wandered out of town into the bush in the direction of some distant drumming. It was night before I reached the place from which it came. Since I had to return in the darkness anyway, I kept going forward. The sound of drums is very deceptive in the night; it always seems much closer than it is. Finally I saw the glimmer of a small fire. Dark shapes huddled around it, half-chanting, half-grunting, watching several others who were manipulating knives over something on the ground. Before I could see what was going on, they became aware of me, and before they moved, the atmosphere stiffened. No word was spoken. There was a moment of sizzling tension. I had trespassed into a black communion of secret ritual. Some of the men loomed large in front of the flames and moved slowly toward me. . . .

I got back to Timbuctoo much quicker than I had come.

When I told Monsieur Bobet about it at the store, he laughed.

"Magic, superstition, ghosts . . . all nonsense," he said. "*Figurez-vous,* when I first came to Timbuctoo, I picked out a house to live in. The commander told me that I could even have electricity. Large, roomy house . . . nice terrace, beautiful view. . . . Well, not much of a view, really, but a nice house all the same. The owner, a Songhaï, said it was fine with him, but—there was a capital But. Everybody else warned me not to go near the place; everybody else said that it was haunted. That's why the rent was so low.

"Haunted! They have a proverb here: 'Don't move into a house before you know why it is empty.' Can you imagine how long it would have taken me to find out from those scatterbrains around here? Anyway, I didn't give a damn about it being haunted. I moved in—quietly, you understand. I didn't want to provoke any horseplay. You never know with these jokers. Do you realize that you can get into trouble if you so much as shy a rock at a stray dog? Can't do it; you might hurt somebody's feelings. You see, the dog might be somebody's cousin, and it wouldn't do to offend a relative whose reincarnation got fouled up.

"As I was saying: I moved in, myself and a bottle of cognac. Nothing happened; quiet as a church all night. I slept like a log. I heard and saw nothing; oh, a rat or two, of course, and a few centipedes, but I don't call that ghosts. I have seen white mice as big as elephants in my day, but I have never been afraid of ghosts.

"I sat up part of the night out of curiosity; maybe that's what made me sleep later than usual.

"Toward morning, I did hear something, something like sneaking footsteps. Frankly, I had got so used to the idea that it was all bunk, I felt a little queer inside when something did happen. I sat up and had a quick one. Then I lit the candle. They were footsteps all right, and they were coming my way. I listened . . . they stopped, but, sure enough, as I looked more closely, I could see the doorknob turning. Mind you, I wasn't afraid, but I didn't like it, either. I got up and tiptoed across the room. I stood there for a minute, then I turned the key and yanked the door open.

"There was a shriek and a body crumbled at my feet.

"So the place *was* haunted, but the ghost had fainted! Why? Because the commander had sent a boy right away to see about the electricity. The boy didn't know that I had moved in. He knew that the place was haunted, and he had taken *me* for a ghost!"

One morning I woke to the beating of drums and the shouting of hundreds of people who were milling around outside. Gaudy Negro women shuffled along in rhythm, wagging their heads and clapping their hands; men were singing and brandishing sticks; camel riders darted in and out of the crowd; there was even a truck, creeping along in low gear, that spilled over with yelling men and children. I learned that this was the celebration of a Songhaï marriage. It continued for four days. The merrymakers circulated all over town; they jammed the streets and finally poured like a flood into the wide square of Baghindé. Meanwhile, in the courtyard of his parents' house, the bridegroom sat in state with a hood over his head, surrounded by his friends who tossed wads of money to the crowd from time to time. The bride was kept under protection by her clan in another house, applauded by a multitude of women from the adjoining rooftops. The climax came with a frenzied battle when the bridegroom's followers attacked the stronghold of the bride and carried her off in triumph.

Then all was quiet again; draped figures strode about silently in the hush of the heat; the wan atmosphere of the ages settled over the ruins, and the closely packed houses in the center of town appeared like a conglomeration of mausoleums.

2   *Yesterday*

THE PERMANENTLY OPEN HOUSE OF MONSIEUR ABDER-RAHMAN Nekli, the director of the Arab college, was the social and intellectual focal point of the city. In the shade of his veranda near the lagoon a wide variety of refreshments was always at hand, and Madame Nekli with the almond eyes supervised the production of delectable dishes. Her husband's profound knowledge and ready wit guaranted a stimulating evening. It was thanks to my conversations with him that I gained a brief glimpse of the complicated history of Timbuctoo.

One wonders if there ever has been a native African city in a normal state of preservation. References of early travelers lead one to believe that they always were partially destroyed or in a lamentable state of disrepair. Richardson's description of Ghat, Barth's account of Agades, Clapperton's report on Kano, all concur, and Timbuctoo is no exception.

It is quite possible that, if Major Joseph Joffre had not occupied the city after Colonel Pierre Bonnier and his hundred men were wiped out by the Tuareg, none of it would be left today, for the town was rapidly disintegrating and the natives were at each others' throats when the French arrived in 1894.

The name is said to be derived from that of a female Bellah slave, Tomboutou, who was left to guard the possessions of her masters when the locality was a Tuareg camp. Another version has it that the name comes from the Songhaï word *toumboutou,* depression (among the dunes). The city proper was founded in the eleventh century and, due to its unique position near the great river where the southern edge of the desert meets the bush, at the dividing line of the nomadic Berber tribes and the sedentary cattle-raising Sudanese, it gradually grew in importance as a trading center, a seat of learning and a den of iniquity. Along with Djenné and Gao, it became a thriving market for the Sahara under the Songhaï empire.

Legends and medieval Arab chronicles suggest that the numerous tribes which became known as the Songhaï emigrated from the east, probably the Nile valley. Despite the presence of the Tuareg, they settled in the region of the middle Niger toward the end of the seventh century, at the time of the first Arab invasion in the north. The Beled es-Sudan, the Land of the Blacks, below the Sahara, was inhabited—among many lesser tribes—by the Bambara, Mandingoes, Mossi in the south, and the Malinkes in the west. None of these indigenous peoples welcomed the newcomers who, nevertheless, had come to stay. At this time, they worshipped a fish who wore a golden ring in his nose, and who appeared above the water at fixed intervals to command the people. One of their chieftains, Dialliaman, boldly speared and killed this fish one day, and Dialliaman became king of the Songhaï, the first of a dynasty of thirty-one "Dias."

The Songhaï empire reached from Djenné in the west all along the Niger bend to the mountains of Aïr in the east, until the powerful Mandingo king of Mali, Kankan-Mussa, took possession of the entire region in one of the most colossal lang-grabs of all time. "A pious and equitable prince," states the Tarikh es-Sudan, "who was unequalled by any other king of Mali in virtue and righteousness. He made the pilgrimage to Mecca in the first years of the 9th century of the Hijirah,* but God knows better than anyone at what exact date." (At the risk of appearing presumptuous, it was in the year 1324.) Upon his return to Timbuctoo, he built himself a lavish palace and gave proof of his religious zeal by founding the great mosque of Dyingerey Ber. Rich merchants and learned men came to join the promising community from Fez, Djenné and Oualata. The first rumors of a city of gold, of a terrestrial paradise in the heart of Africa, were heard in Europe. Kankan-Mussa had no sooner been laid in his grave, eight years later, than the pagan Mossi came out of the southern jungle to sack Timbuctoo. They stayed and enjoyed the spoils for several years until they were driven out by Mussa's successor who, in turn, was defeated by the Tuareg. Their king, Akil, appointed an able administrator under the title of Toumboutou-koy to govern the city to his profit on a basis of business-as-usual. During all this time the Songhaï were vassals to the Mandingoes. By 1468, one of their princes, Sunni Ali, had gathered enough support, and a sufficiently strong army, to attack the city and slaughter anyone who did not side with him, including a large number of skeptical *marabouts*. The turncoats were rewarded and, by chopping off heads right and left, the

---

* The year of the Prophet's flight to Yathrib (Medina), from which the Moslem calendar is reckoned

man who believed in witchcraft, who refused to fast during
Ramadan, who put off his prayers until the morrow and
never bowed or prostrated himself before Allah, who had
women he fancied (married or not) brought to his bed
after the fashion of Louis XIV—this man, the very opposite
of the pious Kankan-Mussa, became master of the Sudan.
He besieged and conquered Djenné but, on hearing that
the chief of the city had died during the siege, and pleasantly
impressed by the youthful son who came forward to negoti-
ate with him, he married the widowed mother on the spot
and refrained from the frightful atrocities which he committed in Timbuctoo. His energy was equaled by Gargan-
tuan tantrums. He had so often condemned his best friends
to death on the spur of the moment that his executioners
sometimes compromised by holding a doomed man in jail
when they felt that the emperor might regret his hasty
decision later. As soon as his mood had changed, they
would let him know that the execution of a particular
person had been deferred. This, usually, made him very
happy and inclined to apologize for his mistake. After a
reign of twenty-eight years, Sunni Ali drowned in a river
during one of his campaigns. His favorite general, Mohamed ben Abou Bekr, who had escaped the emperor's
henchmen on more than one occasion, now engaged Ali's
son in battle and defeated his army after a long and bloody
fight. Ali's followers were aghast when Abou Bekr declared
himself emperor. They voiced their disapproval with loud
cries of *"Askia! Askia!* He Shall Not Be [our chief]!"
Whereupon Abou Bekr, with fine irony, proclaimed that,
henceforth, he would be known as Askia Mohamed—the

Yesterday · 257

first and the most brilliant of the dynasty of all the Askias.

Askia Mohamed conquered the Mossi in the south, the Mali empire in the west, the Hausa kingdoms of Kano and Katsina in the east. From a pilgrimage to Mecca he returned as Askia El-Hadj, the Holy One, and put into effect methods of administration which he had learned in Egypt, selecting the ablest of his hundred sons for important posts as viceroys in the various provinces. This, the sixteenth century, was the golden age of Timbuctoo, when the city became renowned throughout the Moslem world as a center of trade and culture, and as the seat of the university of Sankoré. Askia El-Hadj justly became known as Askia the Great. Timbuctoo grew into a city of one hundred thousand inhabitants.

Among so many sons and relatives, jealousies were bound to end in violence; they soon began to liquidate each other, sometimes for the strangest reasons, as in the case of Askia's nephew, Bankouri. Bankouri succeeded in banishing his illustrious uncle to a small island in the Niger "where the toads jumped all around him," but he, also, became objectionable to his entourage because a domesticated ostrich had a fit every time it caught sight of him. Askia Ishak, whose cruelties fill several pages of the Tarikh es-Sudan, had his sister's son eliminated by a sorcerer who performed a ritualistic execution of his image, thus killing his double, without which a man cannot live. The faith of Islam was accepted, understood and practiced only by a select minority; the mass of the Songhaï people were guided, and are guided still, by their ancient good and evil spirits, the Holé Koara and the Holé Bi, presided over by the all-powerful Irké.

Inevitably, in the course of these family squabbles, a determined outsider appeared to turn the situation to his advantage. Shortly after his daring trek across the Sahara in 1591, aided by the aftereffects of a plague which had ravaged Timbuctoo some years earlier, Pasha Djouder reduced the Songhaï empire to a Moroccan colony, held in check by garrisons up and down the Niger. For two centuries the Sudan was subjected to a rule of merciless exploitation which attracted tens of thousands of adventurers from the north. Hundreds of pashas, greedy and dissolute, followed each other in rapid succession. Timbuctoo became the nucleus of crass intrigues, assassinations, private wars, in which the only constant element was the oppression of the Negroes. In 1640 the city was inundated by a flood. And then the Tuareg again rode down the streets in the dead of night on their tall, white, gangling camels to pillage the town whenever it suited them. The population dropped to twenty-five thousand. Off and on the Tuareg were in control of the city until the Fula drove them out, but the worst calamity was yet to come.

A pompous Toucoulor Negro from Senegal returned from Mecca as El Hadj Omar to dazzle his followers into absolute submission by spurious miracles, religious fanaticism, and the claim that he could render himself invisible. He declared a holy war against all unbelievers and launched a slaughter of infidels on an unprecedented scale. In an open letter to the Moslem inhabitants of N'Dar (the present Saint-Louis in Senegal) he warned:

Now I have the power, and I shall not relent until peace terms are offered by your tyrant [the French] who must submit in accordance with the words of our Master:

Yesterday · 259

"Declare war on all those who neither believe in God nor in the Last Judgment, and on those who do not conform to God's will and that of His Prophet, or those who have received a revelation but do not follow the true path, so that they have to pay the *Djezia* [religious tribute] by force and humiliation."

Children of N'Dar, God forbids you to join them. He has said that you must not mingle with the Christian or the Jew, for he who does is no better than a Christian or a Jew.

With fifteen thousand madmen at his heels, El Hadj Omar fulfilled his divine mission by cutting a bloody trail across the Sudan. In Timbuctoo, for the first and only time, Songhaï, Arabs and Tuareg united to trap and massacre the looting Toucoulor until the streets were choked with mutilated corpses.

During the fifty years preceding the French occupation, the Tuareg were virtually masters of the city. They never lived in it, but hovered around the fringes and made incursions to collect "taxes" or anything else they needed at the moment, from gold, slaves, women and camels to a square meal. The inhabitants were in constant terror of these arrogant visitors and permanently bolted their doors, but when a veiled warrior knocked with his spear, they meekly opened up and satisfied his demands as the only alternative to having their throats cut.

It took several years after the French had established a fort and assured a measure of stability before anyone could venture beyond the city limits. The population among the ruins had shrunk to eight thousand, a miserable lot, cowed by a grisly history and bloodstained ghosts.

3   *Saint and Sinner*

COLONIAL GOVERNORS, MILITARY COMMANDERS, ADMINISTRATORS came to the Sudan, fulfilled their prescribed functions, and disappeared from the scene—transients, sent for fixed periods of duty.

Auguste Dupuis, a provincial Frenchman, became an integral part of the life and legend of Timbuctoo.

The founder of the distinguished African Order of the White Fathers, Cardinal Charles Martial Allemand Lavigerie, had one particular ambition among many others: to establish a mission in Timbuctoo. As early as 1875, he had sent three enthusiastic priests across the Sahara, but they never reached their destination. They were murdered in the desert. Now that French troops were in control of the city, the time had come to try again. Auguste Dupuis, who had been trained at headquarters of the order in Algiers, was fortunate enough to be chosen for the task along with his superior, Father Augustin Hacquard. In the company of two other missionaries, destined for a station at Segou, they embarked for the west coast of Africa, and from there took the safer route up the Senegal and Niger rivers into the interior.

Auguste Dupuis was delighted with Timbuctoo from the start. His fluent command of Arabic and his thorough knowledge of the Koran assured him a respectful welcome among the native elite. There was ample slave labor; the two fathers immediately got to work on the construction of a mission and a clinic. Of the two, the latter proved decidedly more popular.

Father Hacquard became known as Abdallah, the Servant of God; Father Dupuis acquired the nickname Jacob: Yakouba. Père Yakouba soon won the confidence of Arabs and Negroes alike, added Songhaï and Tamachec (Tuareg) to his linguistic accomplishments, and developed a profound interest in the natives, especially female. This, unfortunately, led to embarrassments, because some of the officers at the fort had established prior claims. However, there were enough women to go around, and the good father was by no means a lecher, but a kindly, easy going, virile human being. The girls never complained.

As the years went by and tropical dehydration became more acute, Father Yakouba felt as much entitled as anyone to quench his thirst with a swig of Pernod when the day's work was done. Although Moslems don't drink, this was considered in some quarters as "going native." The adminisitrators of the mission in Algiers got worried. As a precautionary measure Father Yakouba was promoted to take charge of a station in "the snake country": Dahomey. There never was any question about his devotion or his ability. He discharged his duties as efficiently as ever but, when a change of circumstances permitted it, he hurried home, to Timbuctoo.

He loved the people and he loved the place; it didn't really matter to him when one of the new fathers was made superior of the mission. The blackest day of his life came with a note from headquarters which recalled him to Algiers.

He did not wish to disobey, nor could he leave his beloved Timbuctoo. He locked himself in his room and tried to calm his tormented soul. The next morning he walked out of the mission without a word.

If it had not been for a wholesome black girl, he might have become a Niger fisherman in his distress, but Salama took him under her wing and convinced him that he was destined for better things. With his knowledge, she reasoned, he could easily get a job with the administration. And he did. Father Yakouba was given the position of special interpreter.

When he got on his feet again, he married Salama. They bought a house and had many children. Yakouba knew more than any other European about the complexities of native life and rendered invaluable services to the administration. He became director of the revived Arab college, and wrote many excellent papers on the languages and customs of the country. In his later years he was given the post of commander of Goundam, an honor which earned him a very fancy uniform. After doing his duty for two years, he happily returned to his study and to Salama. Perhaps the recognition he valued above all others was his initiation as a citizen of Timbuctoo by the Arab cadi and the Songhaï chieftain of the city. It may have been a coincidence, but the mission declined and it was finally abandoned. In the early thirties William Seabrook wrote a book about *The White Monk of Timbuctoo* in which the emphasis is, quite unfairly, on Pernod.

I was very much interested to see Yakouba's house and appreciated an invitation from the family to visit it.

It stands, unchanged, at the end of a narrow, winding street of sand, next to the one in which René Caillé (the first European to leave Timbuctoo alive) had spent two uneasy weeks in 1828. One of the "White Monk's" daughters, Madame Rougé, led me up a dark staircase to the terrace and into the study. The old-fashioned typewriter was still on his desk, and notes and names were scribbled all over the wall near the window. Shelves were lined with rocks and all manner of odds and ends that he had picked up in the desert; the plumed hat and the gorgeous uniform gathered dust in a homemade closet behind chicken wire. I was given to understand that the family did not hold William Seabrook's memory in high esteem. According to Madame Rougé, he had pestered her father with questions and made him drink too much when he was ill, had misrepresented Yakouba from start to finish and, furthermore, had violated the contract he had drawn up so that the famliy never had received a penny in royalties after the publication of the book. She made no bones about the fact that she did not think much of Americans. Her father, she said, had been so concerned about hurting anyone's feelings that he had burned most of his manuscripts shortly before he died. She told me that he had foreseen the very day, and the exact hour, of his death on January 8, 1945.

He had asked his entire family, his children and grandchildren, to come to his house to say good-by to them. In the course of the night, he awoke repeatedly. Each time he asked about the hour, and each time, he said: "Not yet," and went to sleep again. At four in the morning he sat up and asked for a bowl of milk. He drank it while Salama gently supported him. Then he said: "Let me go," lay down, and quietly passed away.

The faithful Salama died in November, 1954.

Perhaps Père Yakouba's remaining manuscripts, if ever they are published, will shed some light on the rumored secrets of the city.

One morning I was sitting on the veranda of the rest-house when a procession of moody Tuareg issued from the Palace of Justice, followed by a number of black captives carrying leopard skins. A smaller group detached itself and slowly approached our compound. A tall and very hand-some young man, his chest loaded with charms, haughty and self-possessed in the manner of a seasoned Oriental poten-tate, came forward to greet me ceremoniously while his retainers stayed in the background.

This was Marouchet, the chief of the Irraghanaten Tuareg, the last of the great desert raiders, who was being tried by the French authorities on three hundred counts, with pillaging, extortion, arms traffic among the milder accusa-tions against him. He had come from the courthouse during an intermission to talk things over with some of the nobles of the tribe, somber veiled men who looked upon these unaccustomed surroundings with contemptuous eyes.

Aguibou fairly jumped to fetch a camp chair for Marouchet; the subchiefs gathered around him on the floor at the far end of the veranda, toying with the ornate daggers which they wore strapped to their left forearms. Their con-versation was in Tamachec. None of these Tuareg, I learned, spoke Arabic. The predicament in which they found themselves was typical of the conflict between two incompatible cultures. They were not criminals in our sense; there was nothing tough or coarse about them. On the contrary, their behavior was polished and refined. Plundering, to them, was an age-old privilege, a natural condition of their existence. They were totally unaware of having done wrong.

In keeping with their ancient tradition, Tuareg nobles never have done a lick of work, all manual labor being performed by their black slaves. In 1946, a momentous thing happened: all natives within the French Union were made citizens of the Republic by a stroke of the pen in the Ministry of France-Overseas in Paris. Among the Tuareg this had a disastrous effect inasmuch as the serfs suddenly discovered that they had the same civil rights as their masters. The nobles did not see it that way. They continued to uphold their traditional authority.

Marouchet was represented by an African lawyer with a thorough understanding of tribal psychology, but he was up against a European judge who had no comprehension of the vast chasm that separates the medieval evaluation of right and wrong from the abstract legal mind and calculating, factual procedure.

To all appearances, most of the French officials would have preferred to leave the whole thing alone, but they had to do something about it under pressure from those of the victims who invoked their social and legal rights.

Marouchet was visibly baffled to see his world crumbling. He had merely exercised a right which had always been the prerogative of a chief. Far from wishing to impose reprisals, his friends among the administrators were doing all they could to save his face, and to smooth out this embarrassing situation, but the ambitious and impersonal Parisian judge was not impressed by native intricacies and etiquette. To him it was a case of pros and cons according to the letter.

"It is true, is it not, that you stole fifty camels from a man named Hallal?" thundered the judge.

"How can I steal from this man," replied Marouchet, "when the man himself belongs to me?"

"This is no laughing matter! Among many other charges you are on trial for theft!"

"We don't call it that! A thief is a poor man. I am a warrior! I could give you a thousand camels tomorrow if I wanted to!"

At times the meaning of Marouchet's words escaped the judge because the interpreter was too frightened to translate them. When he was accused of lying, Marouchet fired back: "I don't lie! I am a great chief and you are a little hired man! You may be able to abuse my body, but you cannot violate my honor! I have no fear of death. If there is no other way to show my scorn, I shall kill myself, and you will have all my tribesmen against you!"

I learned these things without solicitation from men who took part in the trial during the days when Marouchet and his chiefs sat in my compound between sessions to discuss the incomprehensible situation in which he found himself. He always came to greet me with a strange and melancholy intensity in his eyes. I was sorry that we had no language in common. He was a very impressive man—or was he one of the ghosts who survived among the dust of Timbuctoo? He really belonged to another world. The best he could hope for in this one were years of confinement, and, to a nomad, prison is worse than death.

Paradoxically, Timbuctoo, the most important caravan terminal in the southern Sahara, is an unhealthy place for camels. The natives claim that the water makes them ill, hence they never keep their animals in the vicinity longer than is necessary. By March the camels are in danger of the tsetse fly, the carrier of a highly contagious blood disease called *tabourit* (trypanosomiasis). A camel stricken with this disease is referred to by the natives as *mbouri*. In its early stages, the malady can be recognized by a mangy coat and an evil odor, but recovery from it is very rare. When it does occur, an animal never regains its normal stamina after the illness.

There are few camels within the city itself and, since the nomads make it a point to arrive during the night, one could live in Timbuctoo for years without ever seeing a caravan. As soon as they are unloaded, the animals are watered at the nearest lagoon and then turned out to graze among the thorn trees and thistles in the neighborhood of Abaradyou.

Three to four hundred tons of gum arabic are collected yearly by the nomads in the surrounding bush, but the predominant article of export is, and always has been, salt. When Leo Africanus visited the Sudan in the early years of the sixteenth century, the supply was so scarce that a camel load (four bars) sold for eighty ducats (about one hundred and eighty dollars) in Timbuctoo, and even now the demand is so great that Taoudéni rock salt doubles and triples in value by the time it reaches the far interior or the west coast.

No caravan travels farther south than Timbuctoo; from there on transportation is by donkey, truck, river steamer, or pirogues—native scows made of hollowed tree trunks. Extra care is taken in lacing the bars for export with strips of rawhide, and special artisans mark and decorate the slabs of salt in colored inks with abstract patterns, names of Moslem saints and verses from the Koran. In the retail market the bars are sawed into small squares for sale to individual buyers.

4 Conclusion

MOST OF US HAVE A RECURRING DREAM. IN MINE, I FOLLOW A long, long line of tired, swaying beasts, my eyes glued to the ground, watching the patterns and footprints in the sand as the rear bottom parts of the camels' pads squeeze into accordion folds under the pressure of each step. The fixation produces a kind of timeless hypnosis from which, eventually, I awake with a start when an imaginary camel fly dives with a roar into my ear.

The dream brings back to me the almost unbearable fatigue of the long, hot marches over the glittering sand; the nights, full of foreboding, when the icy wind cut through to our bones; the grandiose wasteland with the incandescent haze along the fringe that made one wonder how a landscape of such delicacy could be so merciless.

It makes me think of our meager fare of gritty rice; of the gentle and polite Deeah, doubled up with pain, lying in the desert far behind us, a minute spot, indistinguishable from the rocks around him; of how I, too, acquired the habit of putting on the right sandal first—for good luck— without questioning the logic of the act; of how frail we were in this immensity when sulphurous streaks of dust came hissing over the ground as the first sign of an approaching storm.

And then I remember the words of Salah, the leader of the *azalaï*, at the end of our journey to Timbuctoo: "*Ouallah,* each time we go on this trip our friends are a little surprised to see us again."

It is enough of a trial to go through this once. Only the hardiest of men, and the least desiring, can make a career of it, for in the desert there is nothing to be had, nothing but the reflection of oneself—which may be blurred by weakness, fear, impatience, boredom, or be clear and strong as that of the nomads who are the masters of this magnificent wilderness.

The word prosperity has no meaning among them. Their greatest joy is life itself, the life of the wanderer with its few pleasant surprises, and the poet's embellishments; life with its hardships, dignified and softened by the wisdom of repose.

Najim was all smiles when he called on me. He was very pleased with the present I gave him—a whole series of presents, including my saddle and what remained of the wooden box.

"Yes," he said in answer to my question about Salah, "he is still here. If you like, we go to see him."

Salah had rolled out his straw mat on the floor of a friend's house. His share of the salt bars that we had brought from Taoudéni was stacked in the yard. He was glad to see us and invited us to have tea with him. After lengthy mutual inquiries about the state of our health, he said: "You know, the night before we reached Erg Lemra, we were really lost, and we were all scared."

This remark was significant, coming from a man like Salah, for it proved that even the experienced guide is respectful of the desert, and that he always enters it with caution, as if he were the first to dare it.

For many centuries, the only trail across the southwestern Sahara has been the unmarked road of the salt caravans.

Camel men rarely discuss tribal politics; they are more interested to know the condition of a certain waterhole, which pasture will be good as a stopping place on a future voyage, or which passage through the dunes promises to be the easiest. They will ask each other: "Did you lose any animals? Did you march any nights without the stars?" They are experts in a difficult profession which is closely bound to the earth, and which demands the best of every man.

On the morning after our visit, Salah started on the six-day trek to drive the camels north to pasture. He was eager to return to the tents of his clan and to join his family.

In March there will be another *azalaï,* another "Gather-

Conclusion · *271*

ing of the Camels," and Salah will be first among the men who guide the caravans across the Sahara.

My motive for going into the desert was nothing more than a compelling inner curiosity. I had nothing to sell, nor did I wish to prove anything. I made no startling discoveries or profitable gains. But I felt honored by the trust and hospitality of the nomads, richer in experience and fully rewarded for my pains in visiting the vast and silent world of the Sahara.

Who would not respect a man like Salah? He was an illiterate camel driver, but what admirable poise and wisdom he had acquired among the lonely wastes and the hot, crinkled hills! The fact that he knew more than the others assured a friendly discipline in the functioning of the caravan. Because his ability was not questioned, he never had to assert himself.

I had shared the hardships of the desert men and found shelter in their frail tents. I had come as a stranger. I left as a friend, deeply impressed by their dignity and their courageous way of life.